DATE DUE

NINETEENTH-CENTURY

THOUGHT: THE DISCOVERY OF CHANGE

Edited by

Richard L. Schoenwald

PRENTICE-HALL, INC.
Englewood Cliffs, New Jersey

A SPECTRUM BOOK

Sources of Civilization in the West
Crane Brinton and Robert Lee Wolff,
General Editors

Richard L. Schoenwald, the editor of this volume,
holds his doctorate from Harvard University, and
is currently Associate Professor of History at the
Carnegie Institute of Technology. He has previously taught at Bowdoin College, Wesleyan University, and the Massachusetts Institute of Technology.
Mr. Schoenwald has contributed numerous articles
to journals and reviews, and is the author of
Freud: The Man and His Mind. He is now at work
on a biography of Herbert Spencer.

ALREADY PUBLISHED

The Crisis of Church & State, 1050-1300, *by Brian
Tierney (with selected documents),* S-102
The English Reform Tradition, 1790-1910, *edited
by Sydney W. Jackman,* S-120
The Enlightenment, *edited by Frank E. Manuel,*
S-121
The Italian Renaissance, *edited by Werner L.
Gundersheimer,* S-128

FORTHCOMING VOLUMES

The Ancient World, *edited by Zelph Stewart*
The Protestant Reformation, *edited by Lewis Spitz*
The Catholic Reformation, *edited by Theodore K.
Rabb*
The French Revolution, *edited by Philip Dawson*

Current printing (last number):
10   9   8   7   6   5   4   3   2

ACKNOWLEDGMENTS

The editor acknowledges the following for their permission to include material in this volume: *The Contemporary Review* for W. R. Greg, "Life at High Pressure," from *Contemporary Review*, XXV (1875), 623-35; Columbia University Press for *Autobiography of John Stuart Mill*, pp. 31-32, 157-58; Doubleday & Co., Inc., for Mill, "The Spirit of the Age," in *Essays on Politics and Culture*, ed. Gertrude Himmelfarb, pp. 3, 4, 6, 19, 20. Copyright © 1962 by Gertrude Himmelfarb; Jack Stillinger and the University of Illinois Press for *The Early Draft of John Stuart Mill's Autobiography*, ed. Jack Stillinger, pp. 187-89; Francis E. Mineka and the University of Toronto Press for Mill, *Collected Works*, ed. Francis F. Mineka, XII, 32; XIII, 434, 543-44; Harper & Row, Publishers, Inc., for Mill, *A System of Logic Ratiocinative and Inductive. Being a Connected View of the Principles of Evidence and the Methods of Scientific Investigation*, pp. 586-89, 602-3, 606-7, 632-33, 641-42; Longmans, Green and Co., Inc., for Mill, *Principles of Political Economy. With Some of their Applications to Social Philosophy*, ed. Sir W. J. Ashley, pp. 756-58, 759, 760-61, 736-64, 948-50; and for *The Letters of John Stuart Mill*, ed. Hugh S. R. Elliot, I, 160-62, 165-67, 236, 289-90; II, 359, 386; J. M. Dent & Sons, Ltd., E. P. Dutton & Co., Inc., and Everyman's Library for Mill, *The Subjection of Women*, pp. 221, 233-35, 239, 260-61; *The New Scholasticism* for Edward L. Burke, S.J., "Karl Marx: Reflection of a Young Man on the Choice of a Career in Life," *The New Scholasticism*, XXXV (1961), 197, 201; McGraw-Hill Book Company, Inc., and C. A. Watts & Co., Ltd., for Marx, *Early Writings*, trans. T. B. Bottomore, pp. 120, 122-23, 127, 155; International Publishers Co., Inc., and George Allen & Unwin, Ltd., for Marx, *Capital. A Critique of Political Economy. The Process of Capitalist Production*, trans. Eden and Cedar Paul, pp. 392 n.2, 449-56, 790-92, 844-47, 862-65, 871-74; International Publishers Co., Inc., for Marx and Engels, *Selected Works*, I, 10-15, 16, 104-5, 185-86; II, 427-29; and for Marx and Engels, *Selected Correspondence 1846-1895*, trans. and ed. Dona Torr, pp. 125, 126, 387; John Murray, Publishers, Ltd., for *More Letters of Charles Darwin*, ed. Francis Darwin and A. C. Seward, I, 4, 61-62, 118-19, 120-21, 123, 367; II, 30, 44; for *Darwin's Life and Letters*, I, 377, 384, 497; II, 239, 301; for *The Origin of Species By Means of Natural Selection or the Preservation of Favored Races in the Struggle for Life*, pp. 461, 464-70; and for *The Descent of Man and Selection in Relation to Sex*, I, 180-81, 182, 191; II, 796-97; Harcourt, Brace & World, Inc., for *The Autobiography of Charles Darwin*, ed. Nora Barlow, pp. 23, 52-53, 76-79, 85-87, 92-96, 118-22, 122-24, 130-31, 139-41, 144-45. Copyright © 1958 by Nora Barlow; The Trustees, British Museum (Natural History), Sir Gavin de Beer, and G. P. Darwin for "Darwin's Notebooks on Transmutation of Species," ed. Sir Gavin de Beer, in *Bulletin of the British Museum (Natural History). Historical Series*, II (1960), 27, 43, 49, 53, 68, 69, 88,

ACKNOWLEDGMENTS

91, 101, 132, 142, 163, 164, 167, 168, 173; Paul H. Barrett, *Centennial Review,* G. P. Darwin, and the Librarian of Cambridge University for Paul H. Barrett, "From Darwin's Unpublished Notebooks," in *Centennial Review of Arts and Sciences,* III (1959), 403; The Linnean Society, London, and the Johnson Reprint Corporation, Ltd., for Charles Darwin and Alfred Russel Wallace, *Evolution by Natural Selection,* ed. Sir Gavin de Beer, pp. 259-63; Sir Gavin de Beer and the Royal Society for Sir Gavin de Beer, "Some unpublished letters of Charles Darwin," in *Notes and Records of the Royal Society of London,* XIV (1959), 35; The Internationaal Instituut voor Sociale Geschiednis, Amsterdam, for two previously unpublished letters from Darwin to Marx and one from Spencer to Marx; Appleton-Century-Crofts, Inc., for David Duncan, LL.D., *Life and Letters of Herbert Spencer,* I, 59-60; II, 76-77, 145-47, 309-10, 327-29; Random House, Inc., and George Allen & Unwin, Ltd., for "On Fortune and Misfortune in History," condensed from *Force and Freedom,* by Jacob Burckhardt. Copyright 1943 by Pantheon Books, Inc.

FOREWORD

The expectancy, the acceptance, of widespread and, in part at least, *planned* and *directed* change in human affairs is, as Professor Schoenwald points out in his admirably succinct introduction to this volume, a very recent thing. Men have always, surely, been aware of change as fortuitous, unplanned, beyond their control, but, as a world-view, the vision of and the faith in change as at least as "real" and as significant as permanence, is hardly more than two centuries old. It is most important for the understanding of the modern world to get into proper focus this concept of the part played by change in our lives. Professor Schoenwald has wisely limited this volume to six very well chosen examples of the range of nineteenth century Western attempts to understand, plan, and indeed predict, some important phases of social, political, and economic change. His running commentaries enable the reader to cover a great deal of ground in a short space. John Stuart Mill, Karl Marx, Charles Darwin, and Herbert Spencer are treated at length. W. R. Greg, still hesitant and doubtful, makes a fine beginning, and Jacob Burckhardt, sure of the cosmological importance—indeed the inevitability—of change but by no means an optimist, makes a very good ending for the nineteenth century, that "Century of Hope." This volume, essentially dealing with what is commonly called intellectual history or the history of ideas, makes a valuable supplement to another volume in this series, Professor Sydney W. Jackman's *The English Reform Tradition, 1790-1910,* which is essentially a study of one specific manifestation of change —political reform.

Crane Brinton
Harvard University
Series Editor

To Audrey

for past, present, and future

CONTENTS

INTRODUCTION

European history had taken a new direction when a British Prime Minister could remark, as Disraeli did in 1867, "Change is inevitable. In a progressive country change is constant."

Europeans who lived before the nineteenth century had never experienced change as an important part of their lives. They thought that a plow was a plow, and could not imagine its becoming obsolete; they thought that a king was a king, and somebody like him would always rule. Greeks and Romans saw change affecting a long series of generations as a great cycle swung slowly through its ever repeating course; one lifetime differed very little from its successor. Christians witnessed the hand of God shaping destiny over the centuries; one month or year or decade resembled another as humanity slowly drew near the end of time.

The thinkers of the Enlightenment were the first men in Western history to debate seriously whether change might take less time than eternity or millennia. Their hope that men might bring about some changes within a single lifetime, and complete a program of change within a few generations, contributed to the two great demonstrations of change with which modern history begins: the French Revolution and the Industrial Revolution.

The eighteenth century speculated about whether change was possible. The nineteenth knew deliriously that it was. Men and nations expected to rebuild their lives entirely: more and more people claimed the right to change as the only birthright worth having. An expanding economy convinced the middle class that a new light had broken upon the world; the only golden age that had ever existed was the age of iron and steel. The working class demanded to know why it, too, could not change its clothes and join the swelling ranks whose gospel had become change. Aristo-

1

crats and conservatives discovered with dismay that they were being shouldered aside because they wanted to keep change a function of the heavens and the aeons, not of human will and sinew.

Trying to make sense out of an inexhaustible rush of novelties, some nineteenth-century thinkers turned to nature, hoping that science might disclose a universal pattern of change. Others turned to history, hoping to sketch a curve revealing where change had come from, how it was accelerating, and where it was heading. Still others believed that only the unchanging furnished a reliable guide, and so they assessed turbulence against the apparent fixity of metaphysical systems.

The six writers included in this book show a wide range of nineteenth-century reactions to change. They differ in many ways, but they all show that change had come to characterize life completely, and that it demanded understanding. They differ considerably—in the social and economic background from which they come, in their conceptions of their roles as investigators of change, in the amount of money and energy at their command, in their fondness for science, in their effect on their own time. Yet in many ways they are bound to each other, by similarities of ideas, sometimes by more personal ties, and above all by their conviction that in a world in which change would never stop, intelligent men had to come to terms with change.

That conclusion links them to the twentieth century, which is discovering how many of its problems arose when men first experienced change as a mass and massive phenomenon. The twentieth century may scorn the nineteenth's fondness for elevating its dearly held wishes into laws allegedly supported by past history and confirmable by history yet to come. But the twentieth century may also envy the determination with which nineteenth-century men tried hard to understand change.

A Note on the Texts

I should like to acknowledge here my indebtedness to those publishers, agencies, and persons who have granted permission to reprint the various selections in this book. A full list of acknowledgments can be found on the copyright page of this volume, and in the footnotes to the individual selections. One editorial practice should be explained. I have used initial ellipsis points only when a selection begins in the middle of a paragraph of the original text. Terminal ellipsis points have been used whenever the original chapter, essay, or letter continues beyond the material quoted here. Internal ellipsis is indicated in the usual fashion.

W. R. GREG

"Life at High Pressure"—its hectic reality and doubts about its value—is the subject of the English essayist W. R. Greg (1809-1881).[1] Born in Manchester, at nineteen he was managing one of his father's mills, and by 1832 was in business for himself. By the early 1840s his talent as a writer was evident in works such as *Not Over-Production, but Deficient Consumption, the Source of our Sufferings,* considered by one authority the best statement by a businessman of his class's attitude to the Corn Laws. His business began to fail, in part because of his preference for writing and reflection, and he gave it up entirely in 1850, when he began to publish extensively. From 1856 to 1877 he held government posts which gave him independence.

In this essay, originally delivered as a lecture at the Royal Institution in London, Greg spoke for many of his contemporaries. Some of his themes recur elsewhere in this collection: in Mill's hope that the classes with advantages may set an example; in Marx's fascination with machinery and with constantly increasing wealth; in the attempts of Darwin and Spencer to connect the individual's biological status with the nation's achievement.

Life at High Pressure

I am only too conscious that I can offer little fitted to occupy the time, or to command the interest of an audience accustomed to be fed on the cream of experimental science, and the inexhaustible wonders of the organic world,—equally conscious that I have nothing original or remarkable to say, even on the subject I propose to treat;—still it may afford something of the refreshment of variety at least to look for a while upon a few of the more

[1] "Life at High Pressure," *Contemporary Review,* XXV (1875), 623-35. Reprinted by permission of *The Contemporary Review,* 36, Broadway, London, England.

peculiar features of the life we are ourselves leading in this age of stir and change; upon some of the probable issues of that hurried and high-pressure existence, and upon the question, not less momentous than individually interesting, how far its actuality corresponds, or could be made to correspond, with the ideal we, many of us, in our higher moments are prone to picture.

It is well in all careers to get occasionally outside of ourselves, to take stock of our acquisitions and their inherent value; to pause in the race, not only to measure our progress, but carefully to scrutinize our direction; and the more breathless the race, the more essential, as assuredly the more difficult and perhaps the more unwelcome, does this scrutiny become.

I

Beyond doubt, the most salient characteristic of life in this latter portion of the 19th century is its SPEED,—what we may call its hurry, the rate at which we move, the high-pressure at which we work;—and the question to be considered is, first, whether this rapid rate is in itself a good; and, next, whether it is worth the price we pay for it—a price rarely reckoned up, and not very easy thoroughly to ascertain. Unquestionably, life seems fuller and longer for this speed—is it truly *richer* and more effective? No doubt we can do more in our seventy years for the pace at which we travel; but are the extra things we do always worth doing? No doubt, we can *do* more; but is "doing" everything, and "being" nothing?

The first point to notice is, that we have got into a habit of valuing speed *as* speed, with little reference to the objects sought by rapid locomotion, or the use to which we put the time so gained. We are growing feverishly impatient in *temperament*. There is nothing to wonder at in this, however much there may be to regret, when we reflect that all the improvement in the rate of travelling achieved by the human race in its orthodox 6,000 years of existence[2] has been achieved in our own lifetime—that is, in the last 50 years. . . .

When our fathers wanted to send a message to their nephews, they could do no better, and go no quicker. When we were young, if we

[2] Greg is referring to the belief once widely held by religious people that the world and man were created in 4004 B.C.

wished to travel from London to Edinburgh, we thought ourselves lucky if we could average eight miles an hour,—just as Robert Bruce might have done. Now, in our old age, we feel ourselves aggrieved if we do not average thirty miles. . . .[3]

Our love of and our pride in rapidity of movement, therefore, are under the circumstances natural enough, but they are not rational sentiments; nor are they healthy symptoms, for they grow daily with what they feed on; and national competition, especially transatlantic competition, stimulates them year by year. Mr. [Matthew] Arnold writes:—

> Your middle-class man thinks it the highest pitch of development and civilization when his letters are carried twelve times a day from Islington to Camberwell and from Camberwell to Islington, and if railway trains run to and fro between them every quarter of an hour. He thinks it nothing that the trains only carry him from a dismal illiberal life at Islington to a dismal illiberal life at Camberwell; and that the letters only tell him that such is the life there.

It is impossible to state more tersely (or more tartly) our indictment against the spirit of the age. . . .

The rapidity of railway travelling, I believe observant physicians tell us, produces a kind of chronic disturbance in the nervous system of those who use it much—a disturbance often obviously mischievous in the more sensitive organizations, distinctly perceptible even in hardier frames. The anxiety to be in time, the hurrying pace—often the running to catch trains (which are punctual in starting, whatever they may be in arriving)—cause a daily wear and tear, as well as accelerated action of the heart, of which, in a few months or years, most of us become unpleasantly conscious, and which, as we all know, sometimes have a fatal and sudden termination (I know three such instances in my own small acquaintance). And the proportion of the population who habitually travel by rail is already large, and is increasing year by year. . . .

The moral effects of this hurried pace cannot well be separated from those arising from the high-pressure style of life generally, but in combination with this are undeniable, if not easy to be specified. A life without leisure and without pause—a life of *haste*—above all

[3] Greg is quoting "Realisable Ideals," an essay in his *Enigmas of Life* (1872), which he cites.

a life of excitement, such as haste inevitably involves—a life filled
so full, even if it be full of interest and toil, that we have no time
to reflect where we have been and whither we intend to go; what
we have done and what we plan to do, still less what is the value,
and the purpose, and *the price* of what we have seen, and done,
and visited—can scarcely be deemed an adequate or worthy life. . . .

We are, perhaps, most of us, conscious at some moments of our
course of the need to be quiet, to be in repose, to be *alone;* but I
believe few of us have ever estimated adquately the degree in which
an *atmosphere of excitement,* especially when we enter it young and
continue in it habitually, is fatal to the higher and deeper life: the
subtle poison which it disseminates through the whole character;
how it saps solidity and strength of mind; how it daily becomes
more necessary and in increasing measure; with what "inexorable
logic" it at once enfeebles and renders abnormally sensitive the
subtle organization of the brain; and how far, by slow and sure
gradations, it carries us on towards a mental and moral condition
which may justly be pronounced unsound. The scenes witnessed
in a neighbouring country during the distressing years of 1870-71
brought out very forcibly these considerations. I may venture to
quote a few paragraphs in illustration, written at the time.[4]

> Among civilised European peoples, the French excitability of to-day
> seems peculiar in kind as well as excessive in degree. . . .
>
> The explanation, I believe, must be sought in physiological consid-
> erations. The wonder would be, looking at the past, if something of the
> kind had not resulted. For three generations Frenchmen have been
> "born in bitterness, and nurtured in convulsion." . . . First, the unprec-
> edented catastrophe of 1789. . . .
>
> Then followed another period of excitement of a different order,
> during which the generation born between 1789 and 1793 had its ado-
> lescence and its nurture. The delirium of triumph succeeded the de-
> lirium of revolution. Every day brought tidings of a fresh victory; every
> year saw the celebration of a new conquest. For twenty years the whole
> nation lived upon continuous stimulants of the most intoxicating sort.
> The Frenchmen born while society was being convulsed, and bred
> while Europe was being subdued, became the progenitors of the French-
> men who witnessed or caused the revolutions of 1830 and 1848; and

[4] *Suum cuique.* Fraser's Magazine, July, 1871, pp. 124-126. [Greg's note.]

these in their turn gave birth to those—still punier and still more demoralised and distempered by the perpetual dram-drinking which public life in France had been—who now stand before the judgment-seat of Europe as the men and women of 1871. For more than ninety years France has scarcely been sane and sober for an hour; ceaseless emotion has grown into chronic hysteria; and defects, vices, and propensities, mental and moral once, have become constitutional and physical at last.

II

But our "life at high-pressure" is shown even more in our style of work than in our rate of movement. The world is growing more exacting in its demands from all labourers except merely manual ones; and life in one way or other is becoming severer and severer to nearly all. The great prizes of social existence—success in professional, public, and commercial life—demand more strenuous and exhausting toil, a greater strain upon both bodily and mental powers, a sterner concentration of effort and of aim, and a more harsh and rigid sacrifice of the relaxations and amenities which time offers to the easy-going and unambitious, than was formerly the case. The eminent lawyer, the physician in full practice, the minister, and the politician who aspires to be a minister—even the literary workman, or the eager man of science—are one and all condemned to an amount and continued severity of exertion of which our grandfathers knew little, and which forces one after another of them to break off (or to break down) in mid-career, shattered, paralysed, reduced to premature inaction or senility. In every line of life we see almost daily examples; for what actual toil does for the learned professions, perpetual anxiety does for the merchant and the manufacturer. The barrister tells us that he must make hay while the sun shines, because for him it generally shines so late; and his career is so often divided into two equal portions— waiting wearily for work, and being absorbed in it—groaning or sinking under its excess. The physician cannot in middle life refuse or select among the crowding patients whom he has looked and longed for through the years of youth, even though his strength is consciously giving way under the burdensome and urgent calls;

while the statesman or the member of Parliament in office has constantly to undergo a degree of prolonged pressure which it is astonishing that so many can endure, and perhaps more astonishing still that so many are found passionately struggling to reach. We all of us remember the description given of this career by one of its most eminent votaries: "There is little reason in my opinion," said Macaulay, "to envy a pursuit in which the most its devotees can expect is that, by relinquishing liberal studies and social comfort, by passing nights without sleep, and summers without one glimpse of the beauties of nature, they may attain that laborious, that invidious, that closely-watched slavery which is mocked with the name of power." . . .

People maintain that this excess of toil is unavoidable, that you must keep the pace, or fall behind and be trampled down by competitors who are more ambitious, more concentrated, or less inclined to measure and appraise the objects and the worth of life; and that in a civilization like ours moderation is forbidden to those who would succeed at all, or not actually fail. It may be so, though I am not quite convinced it is so; and at least, if men must work *over hard,* they need not work *over long;* they might yield the vacant place to younger and needier aspirants. But if it be thus—that it *is* thus is precisely my indictment against the spirit of the age. Excess is enforced; moderation—that which to the wiser Greeks seemed the essence of wisdom—is forbidden, or appears to be so.

But even this is not the extreme limit of the evil to be signalised. Another point seldom enough noticed is that this high-pressure, this ceaselessness and severity of toil, leaves the work of life, and assigns its prizes, more and more to men of *exceptional physique*—the peculiarly healthy, the specially strong, the abnormally tough,—those whose rare frames and constitutions are fitted to endure the unnatural and injurious strain under which the average man succumbs. . . . In short, the race of life is so rapid, the struggle of life so stern, the work of life so hard, that *exceptional organizations* seem to be essential everywhere to great achievement or even ordinary fruits; the moderately-endowed, the steady fair average man, the *medium* in all things—in wealth, in brains, in health and strength—is "nowhere" in the strife. . . .

III

It would seem, again, that the future, in England at least, is not to be for the moderately-wealthy, any more than for the moderately industrious or the moderately clever. There is danger of this in every rapidly progressive country, and the symptoms of it in England have become very manifest of late years. Several operations have combined to produce this result. The aggregate wealth of the country has enormously increased. The profits of *enterprise,* if not of ordinary plodding trade, have been almost unprecedentedly great. More *vast* fortunes have been heaped up, and heaped up in a shorter time, than probably at any former epoch. At the same time the wages of labour, most notably of skilled labour, have increased in many instances 15, 25, even 50 per cent.;—have so increased that if the artisan and mining classes had been prudent, steady, saving, and forecasting, they might, as a rule, have been capitalists as well as labourers now; might have been more at ease in their circumstances, and have had a larger *margin* in their expenditure, than numbers of the educated classes. There is no question as to these facts, and I need not trouble you with statistical details. At the same time, the value of fixed property, of houses and lands, has risen rapidly and largely as a consequence of the general prosperity: more persons are seeking property of this sort, and more purchasers are able and willing to pay a high price for it. In all this, you will say, there is much to rejoice at and nothing to regret. I am not about to controvert this proposition. But let us look for a moment at one or two of the secondary consequences of this state of things.

It is a universal complaint, the substantial truth of which cannot be denied, that life to a vast proportion of the middle classes is becoming more difficult and more costly. . . . Probably, on the whole, we are within the mark if we say that, among average middle-class families, the actual cost of living is 25 per cent. higher than it was twenty-five years ago.

But this is only half the story. Owing to the increasing wealth of the wealthy, and the increasing numbers who every year step into the wealthier class, the *style of living,* as well as the cost of the necessaries and comforts of which "living" consists, [have] advanced in an extraordinary ratio; and however frugal, however unostentatious, however rational we may be, however resolute to live as we think we ought, and not as others do around us, it is, as we all find, simply *impossible* not to be influenced by their example and to fall into their ways, unless we are content either to live in remote districts or in an isolated fashion. The result is that we need many things that our fathers did not, and that for each of those many things we must pay more. Even where prices are lower, quantities are increased. Locomotion is cheaper; but every middle-class family travels far more than formerly. . . . . England is a country in which it is easier to make much than to live upon little; and in which, therefore, the moderate, contented, unstriving natures—those who desire to pass their life neither in making money nor in spending it, who wish to use existence wisely and enjoy it worthily—are in danger of being crushed out of being between the upper and the nether mill-stones of a prosperous and well-paid labouring class and the lavish expenditure of the noble or ignoble opulent.

Now, I confess this does seem to me a matter for regret, inasmuch as these people are, or, at least, used to be, a valuable and estimable element in the national life. I should grieve to see England consist *only* of the toiling, grinding labourer, however highly paid—of the striving, pushing, racing man of enterprise, however successful—and of the plutocrat or aristocrat, however magnificent or stately in his affluence. It may be useless to repine at the menaced operation, and I see but one mode by which it can be effectually counteracted. As wealth increases, and as fortunes grow more and more colossal, as year by year successful enterprise places riches within the reach of many, and as the disposition of every class to imitate and emulate the style of living of the classes above it in the social scale remains about the most inveterate of our national characteristics, there would seem to be small hope of attaining a standard of life truly dignified and worthy, except through such a regeneration in the tastes and sentiments of the opulent and noble—the leaders of fashion, the acknowledged chiefs and stars of society—as should cause simplicity to become "good style," and luxury beyond a certain point, and ostentation at any point, to be voted vulgar. The seeds of this moral revulsion from our actual excesses are already in existence, and a few bright and resolute examples among the well-placed, the eminent, and the universally admired, might, I am convinced, make them germinate with a rapidity that would amaze us; for there are thousands among our upper ranks to whom all the indulgences and splendour round them bring no true enjoyment, but rather the intense sadness of satiety, and not a little self-reproach, and some dim and fruitless yearning after a course of days that shall be more really happy while it lasts, and shall leave more rewarding memories behind it. . . .

Now, I am not given to preaching; I never knew much good come of sermons, and certainly I am not going so far to abuse your patience as to turn this desk into a pulpit. But we may philosophise for a moment, and yet steer clear of moralising. I never had the faintest respect for ASCETICISM, which, indeed, in every shape, I have always regarded as a mistake, arising out of utter misconceptions, both intellectual and moral. I have not even a word to say (now, at least,) in favour of self-denial; that noble virtue has its time and place, but it is out of our province here, where we are dealing with what is rational, not with what is right—not with what duty would ordain, but with what sagacity and enlightened selfishness suggest. We need not ask the affluent and the high in rank to forego any one of the advantages or enjoyments which their vast possessions place within their reach; all that is required is, that they make the most of those advantages, and make those possessions yield them the maximum of real pleasure. . . .

JOHN STUART MILL

James Mill (1773-1836) devoted his life to demolishing what he considered a vast accumulation of fanciful notions about government, economics, psychology, and ethics. He intended that his son, John Stuart (1806-1873), should continue the attack, and he determined to mold him systematically into a collector and weigher of evidence. Only facts and rational calculations, the father believed, could end the grip of the dead past on living men. In his *Autobiography* John Stuart Mill described his training from the age of three in the subjects which absorbed his father.

The younger Mill began his *Autobiography* about 1853 and worked over it until 1870. Here he contrasts the world of his childhood, when men often refused to express changed opinions, with the mid-century temper.[1]

The great advance in liberty of discussion, which is one of the most important differences between the present time and that of my childhood, has greatly altered the moralities of this question; and I think that few men of my father's intellect and public spirit, holding with such intensity of moral conviction as he did, unpopular opinions on religion, or on any other of the great subjects of thought, would now either practise or inculcate the withholding of them from the world, unless in the cases, becoming fewer every day, in which frankness on these subjects would either risk the loss of means of subsistence, or would amount to exclusion from some sphere of usefulness peculiarly suitable to the capacities of the individual. On religion in particular the time appears to me to have come, when it is the duty of all who being qualified in point of knowledge, have on mature consideration satisfied themselves that the current opinions are not only false but hurtful, to make their

[1] *Autobiography of John Stuart Mill* (New York: Columbia University Press, 1924), pp. 31-32. Reprinted by permission of Columbia University Press.

dissent known; at least, if they are among those whose station or reputation, gives their opinion a chance of being attended to. Such an avowal would put an end, at once and for ever, to the vulgar prejudice, that what is called, very improperly, unbelief, is connected with any bad qualities either of mind or heart. The world would be astonished if it knew how great a proportion of its brightest ornaments—of those most distinguished even in popular estimation for wisdom and virtue—are complete sceptics in religion; many of them refraining from avowal, less from personal considerations, than from a conscientious, though now in my opinion a most mistaken apprehension, lest by speaking out what would tend to weaken existing beliefs, and by consequence (as they suppose) existing restraints, they should do harm instead of good. . . .

"The Spirit of the Age"

In 1822 Mill went to work at the headquarters of the East India Company; there he gained considerable experience in establishing and implementing policy as he replied to letters from the Company's agents in India. A severe crisis in his life began about 1826. He found himself plagued by doubts about the value of his father's relentlessly reasonable attacks on the old-fashioned and the unreasonable. Must men exchange society's haphazardness for neatly computable predictability? The discovery of poetry and the world of feeling which it opened to him ended a paralyzing depression. He could still affirm his father's conviction that life should be made more reasonable, and less the result of the past's dictation; but he now realized that reformed social arangements would have to serve a much wider range of human capacities than his father had acknowledged. The letters on "The Spirit of the Age" which he published in 1831 show an awareness of possibilities beyond his father's vision.[2]

The "spirit of the age" is in some measure a novel expression. I do not believe that it is to be met with in any work exceeding

[2] "The Spirit of the Age," reprinted in *Essays on Politics and Culture,* ed. Gertrude Himmelfarb (Garden City, N. Y.: Doubleday & Co., Inc., 1962), pp. 3, 4, 6, 19, 20. Copyright © 1962 by Gertrude Himmelfarb. Reprinted by permission of Doubleday & Co., Inc.

fifty years in antiquity. The idea of comparing one's own age with former ages, or with our notion of those which are yet to come, had occurred to philosophers; but it never before was itself the dominant idea of any age.

It is an idea essentially belonging to an age of change. Before men begin to think much and long on the peculiarities of their own times, they must have begun to think that those times are, or are destined to be, distinguished in a very remarkable manner from the times which preceded them. Mankind are then divided, into those who are still what they were, and those who have changed: into the men of the present age, and the men of the past. To the former, the spirit of the age is a subject of exultation; to the latter, of terror; to both, of eager and anxious interest. The wisdom of ancestors, and the march of intellect, are bandied from mouth to mouth; each phrase originally an expression of respect and homage, each ultimately usurped by the partisans of the opposite catch-word, and in the bitterness of their spirit, turned into the sarcastic jibe of hatred and insult.

The present times possess this character. A change has taken place in the human mind; a change which, being effected by insensible gradations, and without noise, had already proceeded far before it was generally perceived. When the fact disclosed itself, thousands awoke as from a dream. They knew not what processes had been going on in the minds of others, or even in their own, until the change began to invade outward objects; and it became clear that those were indeed new men, who insisted upon being governed in a new way.

But mankind are now conscious of their new position. The conviction is already not far from being universal, that the times are pregnant with change; and that the nineteenth century will be known to posterity as the era of one of the greatest revolutions of which history has preserved the remembrance, in the human mind, and in the whole constitution of human society. . . .

The subject is deeply important: for, whatever we may think or affect to think of the present age, we cannot get out of it; we must suffer with its sufferings, and enjoy with its enjoyments; we must share in its lot, and, to be either useful or at ease, we must even partake its character. No man whose good qualities were mainly those

of another age, ever had much influence on his own. And since every
age contains in itself the germ of all future ages as surely as the acorn
contains the future forest, a knowledge of our own age is the foun-
tain of prophecy—the only key to the history of posterity. It is only
in the present that we can know the future; it is only through the
present that it is in our power to influence that which is to come. . . .

The first of the leading peculiarities of the present age is, that
it is an age of transition. Mankind have outgrown old institutions
and old doctrines, and have not yet acquired new ones. When we
say outgrown, we intend to prejudge nothing. A man may not be
either better or happier at six-and-twenty, than he was at six years
of age: but the same jacket which fitted him then, will not fit him
now. . . .

It is, therefore, one of the necessary conditions of humanity, that
the majority must either have wrong opinions, or no fixed opinions,
or must place the degree of reliance warranted by reason, in the
authority of those who have made moral and social philosophy their
peculiar study. It is right that every man should attempt to understand his interest and his duty. It is right that he should follow his
reason as far as his reason will carry him, and cultivate the faculty
as highly as possible. But reason itself will teach most men that they
must, in the last resort, fall back upon the authority of still more
cultivated minds, as the ultimate sanction of the convictions of their
reason itself.

But where is the authority which commands this confidence, or
deserves it? Nowhere: and here we see the peculiar character, and at
the same time the peculiar inconvenience, of a period of moral and
social transition. At all other periods there exists a large body of
received doctrine, covering nearly the whole field of the moral relations of man, and which no one thinks of questioning, backed as it
is by the authority of all, or nearly all, persons, supposed to possess
knowledge enough to qualify them for giving an opinion on the
subject. This state of things does not now exist in the civilized
world—except, indeed, to a certain limited extent in the United
States of America. The progress of inquiry has brought to light the
insufficiency of the ancient doctrines; but those who have made the
investigation of social truths their occupation, have not yet sanc-

tioned any new body of doctrine with their unanimous, or nearly unanimous, consent. . . .

In the mean time, as the old doctrines have gone out, and the new ones have not yet come in, every one must judge for himself as he best may. . . . The first men of the age will one day join hands and be agreed: and then there is no power in itself, on earth or in hell, capable of withstanding them.

But ere this can happen there must be a change in the whole framework of society, as at present constituted. Worldly power must pass from the hands of the stationary part of mankind into those of the progressive part. There must be a moral and social revolution, which shall, indeed, take away no men's lives or property, but which shall leave to no man one fraction of unearned distinction or unearned importance. . . .

[Men could not bring a new world into being until they understood what really produced change, and this understanding would come only to some men. Mill's search for insight, which characterized his entire life, led him to examine ideas circulating in France: those of Saint-Simon, who wanted an industrialized society directed by industrial and scientific leaders; and of Comte, who saw the history of knowledge as a progression toward scientific, or positive, certainty.

Here, in a passage from the first draft of his *Autobiography*,[3] Mill recalled his search in the late 1820s and early 1830s for a "social science" or sociology that would command the support of knowledgeable men. Mill always relied on increasing the numbers of such men, rather than on converting the masses to new truths.

The increasing realization that he was a man of the nineteenth century led Mill away from some of the ideas in which he had been trained by his father and his father's philosophical mentor, Jeremy Bentham (1748-1832). The apparent absence of wrangling about complexities in the physical sciences struck Mill very forcibly. If society could be made the subject of a science, bickering about the proper course of action for a government or an individual would cease. Students of the physical sciences tested, measured, and drew conclusions; if students of society could proceed in the same way, they could solve the problems emerging as change accelerated. The masses would follow the work of such students as best they could, but complete understanding and agreement on the part of the

---

[3] *The Early Draft of John Stuart Mill's Autobiography*, ed. Jack Stillinger (Urbana: University of Illinois Press, 1961), pp. 187-89. Reprinted by permission of the University of Illinois Press and the editor.

masses would not be necessary in order to control and direct change. Such agreement could never be attained, and to expect it could only mean putting an unconquerable difficulty in the way of dealing with the problems created by change.]

. . . At the time of which I am now speaking the only very strong impression which I received from anything connected with St Simonism was derived from an early writing of August Comte, who then called himself in the title page an élève of Saint Simon. In this tract M. Comte announced the doctrine which he has since so copiously illustrated of the natural succession of three states in every branch of knowledge, first, the theological, second, the metaphysical, & third, the positive state; & contended that social science must be subject to the same law; that the feudal & Catholic system was the last phasis of the theological state of the social science, Protestantism the commencement & the doctrines of the French Revolution the consummation of its metaphysical, & that its positive state was yet to come. This doctrine harmonized very well with my existing notions; I already regarded the methods of physical science as the proper models for political: but one important point in the parallelism much insisted on by M. Comte, had not before occurred to me. In mathematics & physics what is called the liberty of conscience or the right of private judgment, is merely nominal: though in no way restrained by law, the liberty is not exercised: those who have studied the subject are all of the same opinion; if any one rejected what has been proved by demonstration or experiment he would be thought to be asserting no right but the right of being a fool: those who have not studied these sciences take their conclusions on trust from those who have, & the practical world goes on incessantly applying laws of nature & conclusions of reasoning which it receives on the faith not of its own reason but of the authority of the instructed. Hitherto it had not occurred to me that the case would be the same in the moral, social, & political branches of speculation if they were equally advanced with the physical.[4] I had always identified defer-

[4] *The next four sentences ("I had always . . . their united authority.") are written at left, replacing the following earlier text:* My hopes of improvement in these respects had hitherto rested upon the reason of the multitude, improved as I hoped it might be by education. I henceforth saw that this was not the best, & not even a reasonable, hope. Without becoming in the smallest degree less zealous for every practicable increase of the knowledge & improvement of

ence to authority with mental slavery & the repression of individual thought. I now perceived that these indeed are the means by which adherence is enforced to opinions from which at least a minority of thinking & instructed persons dissent; but that when all such persons are as nearly unanimous, as they are in the more advanced of the physical Sciences, their authority will have an ascendancy which will be increased, not diminished, by the intellectual & scientific cultivation of the multitude, who, after learning all which their circumstances permit, can do nothing wiser than rely for all beyond on the knowledge of the more highly instructed. I did not become one atom less zealous for increasing the knowledge & improving the understanding of the man; but I no longer believed that the fate of mankind depended on the possibility of making all of them competent judges of questions of government & legislation. From this time my hopes of improvement rested less on the reason of the multitude, than on the possibility of effecting such an improvement in the methods of political & social philosophy, as should enable all thinking & instructed persons who have no sinister interest to be so nearly of one mind on these subjects, as to carry the multitude with them by their united authority. This was a view of matters which as it seemed to me, had been overlooked, or its importance not seen, by my first instructors: & it served still further to widen the distance between my present mode of thinking, & that which I had learnt from Bentham & my father.

[Inducing men to change was, Mill saw, scarcely easy. In 1829 he wrote to Gustave d'Eichthal:[5]]

. . . You are far ahead of us in France. You have only to teach men what is right & they will do it: they are uninformed, but they are

---

the understanding of the many, I saw that they were never likely to be qualified for judges in the last resort of political any more than of physical truths; that what was wanted was such an improvement in the methods of political & social philosophy, as should enable all thinking & instructed persons, who have no sinister interest, to be of one mind on these subjects, as they are on subjects of physical science: after which the more the intelligence of the general multitude became improved, the more they would appreciate the greater knowledge & more exercised judgment of the instructed & the more disposed they would be to defer to their opinion. [Note by Professor Stillinger.]

[5] John Stuart Mill, *Collected Works*. Vols. XII-XIII, *The Earlier Letters . . . ,* ed. Francis E. Mineka (Toronto: University of Toronto Press, 1963), XII, 32. Reprinted by permission of the University of Toronto Press and the editor.

not prejudiced, & are desirous & eager to learn. Here, the grand difficulty is to make them desire to learn. They have such an opinion of
their own wisdom that they do not think they *can* learn; & they have
too little regard for other people to care much whether they learn or
no, in things which only interest the nation in general, or mankind
at large. . . .

[Democracy by no means guaranteed that men would seek to understand
change and make use of what they learned. Mill admired *Democracy in
America,* by Alexis de Tocqueville, and wrote to him in 1840:[6]]

Among so many ideas which are more or less new to me I have
found (what I consider a very great compliment to the justness of
my own view) that one of your general conclusions is exactly
that which I have been almost alone in standing up for here, and
have not as far as I know made a single disciple—namely that the
real danger in democracy, the real evil to be struggled against, and
which all human resources employed while it is not yet too late are
not more than sufficient to fence off—is not anarchy or love of
change, but Chinese stagnation & immobility. . . .

[Mill worked for the East India Company until 1858, when he retired on
a pension following the Company's dissolution. Company employees could
not engage in politics, a prohibition that resulted from eighteenth-century
attempts to curtail powerful vested interests. India House, however, did
provide Mill with an excellent vantage point from which to observe major
developments in politics, and with leisure to ponder them. Writing to
Robert Barclay Fox in 1842 he was guardedly hopeful as he discussed
some of the advances made in the preceding two decades, including the
end of political disabilities on Catholics (1829), the first considerable extension of the vote (1832), and the advance of Chartism, a movement of
workingmen which had, at first, some middle-class backing in its agitation
for additional political reform:[7]]

. . . As for politics I have almost given up thinking on the subject. Passing events suggest no thoughts but what they have been
suggesting for many years past; & there is nothing for a person who
is excluded from active participation in political life, to do, except
to watch the signs which occur of real improvement in mankind's

---

[6] Mill, *Coll. Works,* XIII, 434.
[7] Mill, *Coll. Works,* XIII, 543-44.

ideas on some of the smaller points, & the too slender indications of some approach to improvement in their feelings on the larger ones. I do believe that ever since the changes in the Constitution made by Catholic emancipation and the Reform Act, a considerable portion of the ruling class in this country, especially of the younger men, have been having their minds gradually opened, & the progress of Chartism is I think creating an impression that rulers are bound both in duty & in prudence to take more charge, than they have lately been wont to do, of the interests both temporal & spiritual of the poor. This feeling one can see breaking out in all sort of stupid & frantic forms, as well as influencing silently the opinions & conduct of sensible people. But as to the means of curing or even alleviating great social evils people are as much at sea as they were before. All one can observe, and it is much, is a more solemn sense of their position, & a more conscientious consideration of the questions which come before them, but this is I fear as yet confined to a few. Still one need not feel discouraged. There never was a time when ideas went for more in human affairs than they do now—& one cannot help seeing that any one's honest endeavours must tell for something & may tell for very much, although, in comparison with the mountain of evil to be removed, I never felt disposed to estimate human capabilities at a lower rate than now. . . .

"Ethology": The Science of Human Nature

The rich diverseness of the training which Mill's father had imposed on him, and the unceasing inquisitiveness of his own mind, convinced him that hopes and dreams could never solve political problems. From the 1820s he had been interested in logic, and by the late 1830s he believed that he had discovered how to join the logic of science, which pursued truth by collecting specific cases and then inducing generalizations from them, to the older logic of a pre-scientific world, which deduced propositions from other propositions.

In his *Autobiography* Mill described the reception of the *System of Logic* which he published in 1843. Here he showed how closely he linked a correct view of the mind and its functioning to the altering of ideas and institutions.[8]

[8] Mill, *Autobiography*, pp. 157-58.

. . . How the book came to have, for a work of the kind, so much success, and what sort of persons compose the bulk of those who have bought, I will not venture to say read, it, I have never thoroughly understood. But taken in conjunction with the many proofs which have since been given of a revival of speculation, speculation too of a free kind, in many quarters, and above all (where at one time I should have least expected it) in the Universities, the fact becomes partially intelligible. I have never indulged the illusion that the book had made any considerable impression on philosophical opinion. The German, or *a priori* view of human knowledge, and of the knowing faculties, is likely for some time longer (though it may be hoped in a diminishing degree) to predominate among those who occupy themselves with such inquiries, both here and on the Continent. But the "System of Logic" supplies what was much wanted, a text-book of the opposite doctrine—that which derives all knowledge from experience, and moral and intellectual qualities principally from the direction given to the associations. I make as humble an estimate as anybody of what either an analysis of logical processes, or any possible canons of evidence, can do by themselves, towards guiding or rectifying the operations of the understanding. Combined with other requisites, I certainly do think them of great use; but whatever may be the practical value of a true philosophy of these matters, it is hardly possible to exaggerate the mischiefs of a false one. The notion that truths external to the mind may be known by intuition or consciousness, independently of observation and experience, is, I am persuaded, in these times, the great intellectual support of false doctrines and bad institutions. . . .

[To end the reign of phantoms and bring on the dawn of reliable knowledge: the *Logic* had a task to accomplish. Mill devoted its last part to "The Logic of the Moral Sciences," and included a chapter meant to show "That There Is, or May Be, a Science of Human Nature."

Mill carefully pointed out that he was not proposing an *exact* science of human nature. He believed that the phenomena of human behavior could be shown to relate to each other in rather regular and generally comprehensible ways. This type of demonstration, that men's conduct usually made sense, was possible only if human actions could be connected to universal laws which ruled men. Some aspects would not be explained.

In astronomy, similarly, the general sweep of the planets could be charted, and astronomy became a science, but it could not be an exact science until a multitude of smaller variations in orbits could be accounted for.

Mill wanted to make sense out of the available data on human behavior by sorting and combining evidence into statements that would be reliably useful because they were connectable to much larger, ultimate laws. The pressing need to understand a rapidly altering world forbade Mill to wait until a full and exact science of human nature became available. He resolved, then, to treat groups of related particular facts as special derivations from ultimate laws whose status as ultimate he had to assume—a status he would then prove by showing how many particular facts could be connected to them.

Mill had embraced the characteristic strategy of the nineteenth century: scrupulous attention to specific and concrete instances, joined to a belief in the grandest laws whose effects supposedly were evident in those instances. Mill had to find a way in which a small number of men could agree on wise courses of action for a world changing with whirlwind rapidity. He believed that the physical sciences showed how to link the particular and the general; he admired their hardheaded attention to real details, and their freedom from polemical strife. As a result, he had no choice but to attempt to portray a science of human nature.[9]]

It is a common notion, or at least it is implied in many common modes of speech, that the thoughts, feelings, and actions of sentient beings are not a subject of science, in the same strict sense in which this is true of the objects of outward nature. This notion seems to involve some confusion of ideas, which it is necessary to begin by clearing up.

Any facts are fitted, in themselves, to be a subject of science which follow one another according to constant laws, although those laws may not have been discovered, nor even be discoverable by our existing resources. Take, for instance, the most familiar class of meteorological phenomena, those of rain and sunshine. Scientific inquiry has not yet succeeded in ascertaining the order of antecedence and consequence among these phenomena, so as to be able, at least in our regions of the earth, to predict them with certainty, or even with any high degree of probability. Yet no one doubts that

[9] *A System of Logic Ratiocinative and Inductive. Being a Connected View of the Principles of Evidence and the Methods of Scientific Investigation* (New York: Harper & Brothers, n. d.), pp. 586-89, 602-3, 606-7, 632-33, 641-42. Reprinted by permission of Harper & Row, Publishers, Inc.

the phenomena depend on laws, and that these must be derivative laws resulting from known ultimate laws, those of heat, electricity, vaporization, and elastic fluids. Nor can it be doubted that if we were acquainted with all the antecedent circumstances, we could, even from those more general laws, predict (saving difficulties of calculation) the state of the weather at any future time. Meteorology, therefore, not only has in itself every natural requisite for being, but actually is, a science; though, from the difficulty of observing the facts on which the phenomena depend (a difficulty inherent in the peculiar nature of those phenomena), the science is extremely imperfect; and were it perfect, might probably be of little avail in practice, since the data requisite for applying its principles to particular instances would rarely be procurable.

A case may be conceived, of an intermediate character, between the perfection of science and this its extreme imperfection. It may happen that the greater causes, those on which the principal part of the phenomena depends, are within the reach of observation and measurement; so that if no other causes intervened, a complete explanation could be given not only of the phenomena in general, but of all the variations and modifications which it admits of. But inasmuch as other, perhaps many other causes, separately insignificant in their effects, co-operate or conflict in many or in all cases with those greater causes, the effect, accordingly, presents more or less of aberration from what would be produced by the greater causes alone. Now if these minor causes are not so constantly accessible, or not accessible at all, to accurate observation, the principal mass of the effect may still, as before, be accounted for, and even predicted; but there will be variations and modifications which we shall not be competent to explain thoroughly, and our predictions will not be fulfilled accurately, but only approximately. . . .

The science of human nature is of this description. It falls far short of the standard of exactness now realized in Astronomy; but there is no reason that it should not be as much a science as . . . Astronomy was when its calculations had only mastered the main phenomena, but not the perturbations. . . .

It is no disparagement, therefore, to the science of Human Nature, that those of its general propositions which descend sufficiently into detail to serve as a foundation for predicting phenomena in the con-

crete, are for the most part only approximately true. But in order to give a genuinely scientific character to the study, it is indispensable that these approximate generalizations, which in themselves would amount only to the lowest kind of empirical laws, should be connected deductively with the laws of nature from which they result; should be resolved into the properties of the causes on which the phenomena depend. In other words, the science of Human Nature may be said to exist in proportion as the approximate truths, which compose a practical knowledge of mankind, can be exhibited as corollaries from the universal laws of human nature on which they rest; whereby the proper limits of those approximate truths would be shown, and we should be enabled to deduce others for any new state of circumstances, in anticipation of specific experience. . . .

[There would be a new science of individual man because there had to be. Rules of thumb might guide a generation seeking conditions that would permit change. Far more sophisticated formulations were necessary for an age accustomed to change as a fact and bedeviled by its inability to control and direct change. There is a very good possibility of learning how to shape human behavior in some important ways: that is the impact of the following passage.

Mill's wish to understand how men could be changed led him to venture beyond his more cautious earlier view of the scientific status of knowledge of human action. He announced the creation of an *exact* science, but whether one needed the backing of a universal law to affirm that "an interest on one side of a question tends to bias the judgment" may surely be doubted.

Only by overlooking the ignorance and complacency of many men in Mill's time, however, can one feel surprised that Mill was able to convince himself that a new and exact science had been created so suddenly. Actually Mill was urging that such a science be created, and trying to show as persuasively as he could that, indeed, it could be created without delay. He had to associate himself with the power of the laws of science to undermine the immovable multitudes whose interests lay entrenched on a single side of so many questions. His resemblance here to Marx is very strong.]

A science is thus formed, to which I would propose to give the name of Ethology, or the Science of Character, from ἦθος, a word more nearly corresponding to the term "character" as I here use it, than any other word in the same language. The name is perhaps etymologically applicable to the entire science of our mental and normal nature; but if, as is usual and convenient, we employ the name Psychology for the science of the elementary laws of mind, Ethology will serve for the ulterior science which determines the kind of character produced in conformity to those general laws by any set of circumstances, physical and moral. According to this definition, Ethology is the science which corresponds to the art of education in the widest sense of the term, including the formation of national or collective character as well as individual. It would indeed be vain to expect (however completely the laws of the formation of character might be ascertained) that we could know so accurately the circumstances of any given case as to be able positively to predict the character that would be produced in that case. But we must remember that a degree of knowledge far short of the power of actual prediction is often of much practical value. There may be great power of influencing phenomena, with a very imperfect knowledge of the causes by which they are in any given instance determined. It is enough that we know that certain means have a *tendency* to produce a given effect, and that others have a tendency to frustrate it. When the circumstances of an individual or of a nation are in any considerable degree under our control, we may, by our knowledge of tendencies, be enabled to shape those circumstances in a manner much more favorable to the ends we desire, than the shape which they would of themselves assume. This is the limit of our power; but within this limit the power is a most important one.

This science of Ethology may be called the Exact Science of Human Nature; for its truths are not, like the empirical laws which depend on them, approximate generalizations, but real laws. It is, however (as in all cases of complex phenomena), necessary to the exactness of the propositions, that they should be hypothetical only, and affirm tendencies, not facts. They must not assert that something will always, or certainly, happen; but only that such and such will be the effect of a given cause, so far as it operates uncounteracted. It is a scientific proposition, that bodily strength tends to make men courageous; not that it always makes them so: that an interest on one side of a question tends to bias the judgment; not that it invariably does so: that experience tends to give wisdom; not that such is always its effect. These propositions, being assertive only of tendencies, are not the less universally true because the tendencies may be frustrated.

[Ethology would open the way at last to a real science of men in their relations with each other, a reliable sociology:]

Next after the science of individual man comes the science of man in society—of the actions of collective masses of mankind, and the various phenomena which constitute social life. . . .

All phenomena of society are phenomena of human nature, generated by the action of outward circumstances upon masses of human beings; and if, therefore, the phenomena of human thought, feeling, and action are subject to fixed laws, the phenomena of society can not but conform to fixed laws, the consequence of the preceding. There is, indeed, no hope that these laws, though our knowledge of them were as certain and as complete as it is in astronomy, would enable us to predict the history of society, like that of the celestial appearances, for thousands of years to come. But the difference of certainty is not in the laws themselves, it is in the data to which these laws are to be applied. In astronomy the causes influencing the result are few, and change little, and that little according to known laws; we can ascertain what they are now, and thence determine what they will be at any epoch of a distant future. The data, therefore, in astronomy are as certain as the laws themselves. The circumstances, on the contrary, which influence the condition and progress of society are innumerable, and perpetually changing; and though they all change in obedience to causes, and therefore to laws, the multitude of the causes is so great as to defy our limited powers of calculation. Not to say that the impossibility of applying precise numbers to facts of such a description would set an impassable limit to the possibility of calculating them beforehand, even if the powers of the human intellect were otherwise adequate to the task.

But, as before remarked, an amount of knowledge quite insufficient for prediction, may be most valuable for guidance. The science of society would have attained a very high point of perfection if it enabled us, in any given condition of social affairs, in the condition, for instance, of Europe or any European country at the present time, to understand by what causes it had, in any and every particular, been made what it was; whether it was tending to any, and to what, changes; what effects each feature of its existing state was likely to produce in the future; and by what means any of those effects might be prevented, modified, or accelerated, or a different class of effects superinduced. There is nothing chimerical in the hope that general laws, sufficient to enable us to answer these various questions for any country or time with the individual circumstances of which we are well acquainted, do really admit of being ascertained; and that the other branches of human knowledge, which this undertaking presupposes, are so far advanced that the time is ripe for its commencement. Such is the object of the Social Science. . . .

[Nineteenth-century thinkers characteristically used two methods for making sense out of the unending parade of novelties passing before them. They sought laws so general that any specific example of change would have to be considered and understood in terms of a general law, precisely because the law was so general; and they attempted to gather as much data as they could, to bolster their confidence in the universal truth of these laws, without which they felt unable to bring order into the rapidly increasing mass of information about particular examples of change.

In addition to relying on law, nineteenth-century explorers of change used a second major method for appraising change. They believed that the generations which had peopled the earth up to recent times had scarcely changed at all. Around 1800 men began to change; the amount by which one generation differed from its predecessor increased steadily, and an infinite future would see ever wider distance between generations. For these thinkers, men did not stand still: they developed, or, in a favorite phrase, they progressed. A later generation might differ from an earlier, and the difference might not be judged an improvement, but that possibility was not very likely. As men went onward, they would tend, on the whole, to go upward.

In the following passage Mill attempts to join the methods most widely used by his contemporaries. What he wants is a general law of progress —general because it will have been formed by combining other general laws about the functioning of the mind and the formation of character; concerned with progress because the newness of the world for each successive generation is the fundamental experience of nineteenth-century men. By contrast, the notions of law and progress for eighteenth-century thinkers had a much more questioning and problematic ring: *could* there be change so widespread that two generations would really have difficulty in understanding each other? *Could* laws capture the mysterious secret of the workings and tendency of change? The nineteenth century knew the distance between the generations, as Mill's own experience showed; and it trusted in the existence of laws which would justify change by making its stresses as well as its gains both right and necessary.]

The words Progress and Progressiveness are not here to be understood as synonymous with improvement and tendency to improvement. It is conceivable that the laws of human nature might determine, and even necessitate, a certain series of changes in man and society, which might not in every case, or which might not on the whole, be improvements. It is my belief, indeed, that the general tendency is, and will continue to be, saving occasional and temporary exceptions, one of improvement; a tendency toward a better and happier state. This, however, is not a question of the method of the social science, but a theorem of the science itself. For our purpose it is sufficient that there is a progressive change both in the character of the human race and in their outward circumstances, so far as moulded by themselves; that in each successive age the principal phenomena of society are different from what they were in the age preceding, and still more different from any previous age: the periods which most distinctly mark these successive changes being intervals of one generation, during which a new set of human beings have been educated, have grown up from childhood, and taken possession of society.

The progressiveness of the human race is the foundation on which a method of philosophizing in the social science has been of late years erected. . . . This method, which is now generally adopted by the most advanced thinkers on the Continent, consists in attempting, by a study and analysis of the general facts of history, to discover (what these philosophers term) the law of progress: which law, once ascertained, must according to them enable us to predict future events, just as after a few terms of an infinite series in algebra we are able to detect the principle of regularity in their formation, and to predict the rest of the series to any number of terms we please. The principal aim of historical speculation in France, of late years, has has been to ascertain this law. But while I gladly acknowledge the great services which have been rendered to historical knowledge by this school, I can not but deem them to be mostly chargeable with a fundamental misconception of the true method of social philosophy. The misconception consists in supposing that the order of succession which we may be able to trace among the different states of society and civilization which history presents to us, even if that order were more rigidly uniform than it has yet been proved to be, could ever amount to a law of nature. It can only be an empirical law. The succession of states of the human mind and of human society can not have an independent law of its own; it must depend on the psychological and ethological laws which govern the action of circumstances on men and of men on circumstances. It is conceivable that those laws might be such, and the general circumstances of the human race such, as to determine the successive transformations of man and society to one given and unvarying order. But even if the case were so, it can not be the ultimate aim of science to discover an empirical law. Until that law could be connected with the psychological and ethological laws on which it must depend, and, by the consilience of deduction *a priori* with historical evidence, could be converted from an empirical law into a scientific one, it could not be relied on for the prediction of future events, beyond, at most, strictly adjacent cases. M. Comte alone, among the new historical school, has seen the necessity of thus connecting all our generalizations from history with the laws of human nature.

[Mill's combination of general laws yielding further conclusions by deduction, and the testing of these propositions on evidence from past and present, led him to discover a single, satisfyingly simple key to human development. The key had been shaped as all such keys are—in the movement of his own life and thought. It could scarcely have been an accident that a man as reasonable and inquisitive as Mill should decide that capacities for reasonableness and inquiry determine what an age can achieve. Taking account of the origin of a concept, however, does not demonstrate its usefulness or error. For Mill and for those interested in solving the problems which he faced, the question remains: what could he do with the key whose discovery he announced?]

Now, the evidence of history and that of human nature combine, by a striking instance of consilience, to show that there really is one social element which is thus predominant, and almost paramount, among the agents of the social progression. This is, the state of the speculative faculties of mankind; including the nature of the beliefs which by any means they have arrived at, concerning themselves and the world by which they are surrounded.

It would be a great error, and one very little likely to be committed, to assert that speculation, intellectual activity, the pursuit of truth, is among the more powerful propensities of human nature, or holds a predominating place in the lives of any, save decidedly exceptional, individuals. But, notwithstanding the relative weakness of this principle among other sociological agents, its influence is the main determining cause of social progress; all the other dispositions of our nature which contribute to that progress being dependent on it for the means of accomplishing their share of the work. Thus (to take the most obvious case first), the impelling force to most of the improvements effected in the arts of life, is the desire of increased material comfort; but as we can only act upon external objects in proportion to our knowledge of them, the state of knowledge at any time is the limit of the industrial improvements possible at that time; and the progress of industry must follow, and depend on, the progress of knowledge. The same thing may be shown to be true, though it is not quite so obvious, of the progress of the fine arts. Further, as the strongest propensities of uncultivated or half-cultivated human nature (being the purely selfish ones, and those of a sympathetic character which partake most of the nature of selfishness) evidently tend in themselves to disunite mankind, not to unite them —to make them rivals, not confederates, social existence is only possible by a disciplining of those more powerful propensities, which consists in subordinating them to a common system of opinions. The degree of this subordination is the measure of the completeness of the social union, and the nature of the common opinions determines its kind. But in order that mankind should conform their actions to any set of opinions, these opinions must exist, must be believed by them. And thus, the state of the speculative faculties, the character of the propositions assented to by the intellect, essentially determines the moral and political state of the community, as we have already seen that it determines the physical.

These conclusions, deduced from the laws of human nature, are in entire accordance with the general facts of history. Every considerable change historically known to us in the condition of any portion of mankind, when not brought about by external force, has been preceded by a change, of proportional extent, in the state of their knowledge, or in their prevalent beliefs. As between any given state of speculation, and the correlative state of every thing else, it was almost always the former which first showed itself; though the effects, no doubt, reacted potently upon the cause. Every considerable advance in material civilization has been preceded by an advance in knowledge: and when any great social change has come to pass, either in the way of gradual development or of sudden conflict, it has had for its precursor a great change in the opinions and modes of thinking of society. Polytheism, Judaism, Christianity, Protestantism, the critical philosophy of modern Europe, and its positive science—each of these has been a primary agent in making society what it was at each successive period, while society was but secondarily instrumental in making *them,* each of them (so far as causes can be assigned for its existence) being mainly an emanation not from the practical life of the period, but from the previous state of belief and thought. The weakness of the speculative propensity in mankind generally has not, therefore, prevented the progress of speculation from governing that of society at large; it has only, and too often, prevented progress altogether, where the intellectual progression has come to an early stand for want of sufficiently favorable circumstances.

From this accumulated evidence, we are justified in concluding, that the order of human progression in all respects will mainly depend on the order of progression in the intellectual convictions of mankind, that is, on the law of the successive transformations of human opinions. The question remains, whether this law can be determined; at first from history as an empirical law, then converted into a scientific theorem by deducing it *a priori* from the principles of human nature. As the progress of knowledge and the changes in the opinions of mankind are very slow, and manifest themselves in a well-defined manner only at long intervals, it can not be expected that the general order of sequence should be discoverable from the examination of less than a very considerable part of the duration of the social progress. It is necessary to take into consideration the whole of past time, from the first recorded condition of the human race, to the memorable phenomena of the last and present generations.

Political Economy *and Practical Reform*

Mill soon realized that ethology would have to remain a hope for a very long time. Both his conscience and his intelligence led him to turn to doing what he could about urgent social questions in an enlightened and informed spirit. Mill's plan for a new science dealing with how circumstances make men, and how men react on circumstances, had to fail because there existed as yet too little reliable information from which reliable propositions could be synthesized.

Far from despairing, Mill resolutely devoted the rest of his life to dealing with particular problems in particular, piecemeal ways to the very best of his extraordinary ability. He rebelled against the widespread belief that the laws of economics inexorably condemned thousands to misery. In his *Principles of Political Economy,* first published in 1848, he attempted to show that the laws regulating production are fixed, but that distribution depends on customs and institutions which men can change. The ways in which working men existed could no longer be overlooked, and their claim to a more truly human life could no longer be denied.[10]

Of the working men, at least in the more advanced countries of Europe, it may be pronounced certain, that the patriarchal or paternal system of government is one to which they will not again be subject. That question was decided, when they were taught to read, and allowed access to newspapers and political tracts; when dissenting preachers were suffered to go among them, and appeal to their faculties and feelings in opposition to the creeds professed and countenanced by their superiors; when they were brought together in numbers, to work socially under the same roof; when railways enabled them to shift from place to place, and change their patrons and employers as easily as their coats; when they were encouraged to seek a share in the government, by means of the

[10] *Principles of Political Economy. With Some of their Applications to Social Philosophy,* ed. Sir W. J. Ashley (New York: Longmans, Green and Co., 1909), pp. 756-58, 760-61, 763-64, 948-50, 759. Reprinted by permission of Longmans, Green and Co., Inc. Ashley reprints the seventh edition (1871), and indicates all important earlier variants in footnotes. Ashley's footnotes have been omitted, with one exception.

electoral franchise. The working classes have taken their interests into their own hands, and are perpetually showing that they think the interests of their employers not identical with their own, but opposite to them. Some among the higher classes flatter themselves that these tendencies may be counteracted by moral and religious education: but they have let the time go by for giving an education which can serve their purpose. The principles of the Reformation have reached as low down in society as reading and writing, and the poor will not much longer accept morals and religion of other people's prescribing. . . .

It is on a far other basis that the well-being and well-doing of the labouring people must henceforth rest. The poor have come out of leading-strings, and cannot any longer be governed or treated like children. To their own qualities must now be commended the care of their destiny. . . .

There is no reason to believe that prospect other than hopeful. The progress indeed has hitherto been, and still is, slow. But there is a spontaneous education going on in the minds of the multitude, which may be greatly accelerated and improved by artificial aids. The instruction obtained from newspapers and political tracts may not be the most solid kind of instruction, but it is an immense improvement upon none at all.[11] What it does for a people has been admirably exemplified during the cotton crisis, in the case of the Lancashire spinners and weavers, who have acted with the consistent good sense and forbearance so justly applauded, simply because, being readers of newspapers, they understood the causes of the calamity which had befallen them, and knew that it was in no way imputable either to their employers or to the Government. It is not certain that their conduct would have been as rational and exemplary, if the distress had preceded the salutary measure of fiscal emancipation which gave existence to the penny press. . . .

[In the first edition of his *Principles* Mill had objected strongly to socialism as it was then being discussed. In the third edition (1852) he took a more favorable attitude, limiting his objections to doubts about the moral fitness of the working classes. Mill did believe that some form of

[11] Ashley notes that Mill inserted the next two sentences in the sixth edition (1865). The American Civil War had affected the English textile industry very severely.

cooperation among workers was coming, as his alterations in the last lines of the following excerpts show. What that form would look like was, however, never very clear, and his views on socialism were too idiosyncratic to be labeled at all firmly.]

The political consequences of the increasing power and importance of the operative classes, and of the growing ascendancy of numbers, which, even in England and under the present institutions, is rapidly giving to the will of the majority at least a negative voice in the acts of government, are too wide a subject to be discussed in this place. But, confining ourselves to economical considerations, and notwithstanding the effect which improved intelligence in the working classes, together with just laws, may have in altering the distribution of the produce to their advantage, I cannot think that they will be permanently contented with the condition of labouring for wages as their ultimate state. . . . If the rich regard the poor, as by a kind of natural law, their servants and dependents, the rich in their turn are regarded as a mere prey and pasture for the poor. . . . The total absence of regard for justice or fairness in the relations between the two, is as marked on the side of the employed as on that of the employers. We look in vain among the working classes in general for the just pride which will choose to give good work for good wages; for the most part, their sole endeavour is to receive as much, and return as little in the shape of service, as possible. It will sooner or later become insupportable to the employing classes, to live in close and hourly contact with persons whose interests and feelings are in hostility to them. . . .

The aim of improvement should be not solely to place human beings in a condition in which they will be able to do without one another, but to enable them to work with or for one another in relations not involving dependence. Hitherto there has been no alternative for those who lived by their labour, but that of labouring either each for himself alone, or for a master. But the civilizing and improving influences of association, and the efficiency and economy of production on a large scale, may be obtained without dividing the producers into two parties with hostile interests and feelings, the many who do the work being mere servants under the command of the one who supplies the funds, and having no inter-

est of their own in the enterprise except to earn their wages with
as little labour as possible. The speculations and discussions of the
last fifty years, and the events of the last thirty, are abundantly
conclusive on this point. If the improvement which even trium-
phant military despotism has only retarded, not stopped, shall continue its course, there can be little doubt that the *status* of hired
labourers will gradually tend to confine itself to the description of
workpeople whose low moral qualities render them unfit for anything more independent: and that the relation of masters and workpeople will be gradually superseded by partnership, in one of two
forms: in some cases, association of the labourers with the capitalist;
in others, and perhaps finally in all,[12] association of labourers
among themselves.

[Toward the close of his *Principles* Mill turned to a discussion "Of the
Grounds and Limits of the Laisser-Faire or Non-Interference Principle."
No one has ever affirmed more strongly or with greater conviction the
nineteenth century's belief that men freed to direct their own lives would
learn by doing: the activity of intelligent men promoted intelligence, and
so men would decide intelligently how to adapt to a changing world.
Mill did allow some exceptions to his conviction that governments should
not interfere: in providing education and public services, and in producing changes which individuals could not bring about by themselves, as in
restricting the hours of work.]

I have reserved for the last place one of the strongest of the reasons against the extension of government agency. Even if the government could comprehend within itself, in each department, all
the most eminent intellectual capacity and active talent of the nation, it would not be the less desirable that the conduct of a large
portion of the affairs of the society should be left in the hands of
the persons immediately interested in them. The business of life is
an essential part of the practical education of a people; without
which, book and school instruction, though most necessary and
salutary, does not suffice to qualify them for conduct, and for the
adaptation of means to ends. Instruction is only one of the desid-

---

[12] In 3rd ed.: "temporarily and in some cases . . . , in other cases and finally
in all." In 5th ed. (1862): "perhaps finally in all." In 6th ed. (1865), "temporarily"
omitted. [Ashley's note.]

erata of mental improvement; another, almost as indispensable, is a vigorous exercise of the active energies; labour, contrivance, judgment, self-control: and the natural stimulus to these is the difficulties of life. This doctrine is not to be confounded with the complacent optimism, which represents the evils of life as desirable things, because they call forth qualities adapted to combat with evils. It is only because the difficulties exist, that the qualities which combat with them are of any value. As practical beings it is our business to free human life from as many as possible of its difficulties, and not to keep up a stock of them as hunters preserve game for the exercise of pursuing it. But since the need of active talent and practical judgment in the affairs of life can only be diminished, and not, even on the most favourable supposition, done away with, it is important that those endowments should be cultivated not merely in a select few, but in all, and that the cultivation should be more varied and complete than most persons are able to find in the narrow sphere of their merely individual interests. A people among whom there is no habit of spontaneous action for a collective interest—who look habitually to their government to command or prompt them in all matters of joint concern—who expect to have everything done for them, except what can be made an affair of mere habit and routine—have their faculties only half developed; their education is defective in one of its most important branches.

Not only is the cultivation of the active faculties by exercise, diffused through the whole community, in itself one of the most valuable of national possessions: it is rendered, not less, but more necessary, when a high degree of that indispensable culture is systematically kept up in the chiefs and functionaries of the state. There cannot be a combination of circumstances more dangerous to human welfare, than that in which intelligence and talent are maintained at a high standard within a governing corporation, but starved and discouraged outside the pale. Such a system, more completely than any other, embodies the idea of despotism, by arming with intellectual superiority as an additional weapon those who have already the legal power. It approaches as nearly as the organic difference between human beings and other animals admits, to the government of sheep by their shepherd without anything like so strong an interest as the shepherd has in the thriving condition of the flock. The only security against political slavery is the check maintained over governors by the diffusion of intelligence, activity, and public spirit among the governed. Experience proves the extreme difficulty of permanently keeping up a sufficiently high standard of those qualities; a difficulty which increases, as the advance of civilization and security removes one after another of the hardships, embarrassments, and dangers against which individuals had formerly no resource but in their own strength, skill, and courage. It is therefore of supreme importance that all classes of the community, down to the lowest, should have much to do for themselves; that as great a demand should be made upon their intelligence and virtue as it is in any respect equal to; that the government should not only leave as far as possible to their own faculties the conduct of whatever concerns themselves alone, but should suffer them, or rather encourage them, to manage as many as possible of their joint concerns by voluntary co-operation; since this discussion and management of collective interests is the great school of that public spirit, and the great source of that intelligence of public affairs, which are always regarded as the distinctive character of the public of free countries.

A democratic constitution, not supported by democratic institutions in detail, but confined to the central government, not only is not political freedom, but often creates a spirit precisely the reverse, carrying down to the lowest grade in society the desire and ambition of political domination. In some countries the desire of the people is for not being tyrannized over, but in others it is merely for an equal chance to everybody of tyrannizing. Unhappily this last state of the desires is fully as natural to mankind as the former, and in many of the conditions even of civilized humanity is far more largely exemplified. In proportion as the people are accustomed to manage their affairs by their own active intervention, instead of leaving them to the government, their desires will turn to repelling tyranny, rather than to tyrannizing: while in proportion as all real initiative and direction resides in the government, and individuals habitually feel and act as under its perpetual tutelage, popular institutions develop in them not the desire of freedom, but an unmeasured appetite for place and power; diverting the intelligence and activity of the country from its principal business to a wretched competition for the selfish prizes and the petty vanities of office.

[Mill was probably the first important male thinker in the West to see women as whole human beings, and not as fragmented players of a limited number of roles: sexual object, mother, decorative hostess, exploited worker. He tried to change the preoccupation of thinkers with "men" as a synonym for "man" because he sympathized deeply with suffering human beings, and because the suffering of one woman in particular touched him closely. He had for twenty years loved a woman who was already married. Harriet Taylor would not leave her husband because she feared the scandal that would follow, and Mill married her only after her husband's death in 1851.]

It appears to me impossible but that the increase of intelligence, of education, and of the love of independence among the working classes, must be attended with the corresponding growth of the good sense which manifests itself in provident habits of conduct, and that population, therefore, will bear a gradually diminishing ratio to capital and employment. This most desirable result would be much accelerated by another change, which lies in the direct line of the best tendencies of the time; the opening of industrial occupations freely to both sexes. The same reasons which make it no longer necessary that the poor should depend on the rich, make it equally unnecessary that women should depend on men; and the least which justice requires is that law and custom should not enforce dependence (when the correlative protection has become superfluous) by ordaining that a woman, who does not happen to have a provision by inheritance, shall have scarcely any means open to her of gaining a livelihood, except as a wife and mother. Let women who prefer that occupation, adopt it; but that there should be no option, no other *carrière* possible for the great majority of women, except in the humbler departments of life, is a flagrant social injustice. . . .

[Mill's concern with change extended to the limits of his energy. It was evident not merely in books like the treatise on economics, but in more direct attempts to gain a hearing for his views. Here is a letter to Sir George Grey, at the time the Home Secretary. Mill was sent in return only an official acknowledgment that the letter had been received.[13]]

[13] *The Letters of John Stuart Mill,* ed. Hugh S. R. Elliot (New York: Longmans, Green and Co., 1910), I, 160-62. Reprinted by permission of the publisher.

15th May 1851.

Sir,—I hope I may be pardoned for addressing to you in this form rather than through the newspapers a remonstrance against the gross insult to every woman in the country which has found its way into the Government Bill now passing through the House of Commons for regulating the sale of arsenic. The clause, which did not form part of the Bill as it came from the hands of its framers, but was added in the House of Lords at the suggestion of some unknown person, is that which forbids arsenic to be sold in less quantity than ten pounds to any person "other than a male person of full age," all women, from the highest to the lowest, being declared unfit to have poison in their possession lest they shall commit murder. It is impossible to believe that so monstrous a proposition could have obtained the assent of Government except through inadvertence; and an individual, though personally unknown to you, may hope to be excused if, at the hazard of being thought intrusive, he takes such means as are in his power of soliciting from you that attention to the subject which, he is persuaded, cannot yet have been given to it.

If the Bill passes with this clause, it is a retrograde step in legislation, and a return to the ideas and practices of barbarous ages. One of the characteristics of the improved spirit of the present time is the growing tendency to the elevation of women, towards their relief from disabilities, their increased estimation, the assignment to them of a higher position, both social and domestic. But this clause is a blind step in the wrong direction. It singles out women for the purpose of degrading them. It establishes a special restriction, a peculiar disqualification against them alone. It assumes that women are more addicted than men to committing murder! Does the criminal calendar, or the proceedings of the police courts, show a preponderance of women among the most atrocious criminals? Everybody knows that the direct contrary is the truth, and that men outnumber women in the records of crime in the ratio of four to one. On what supposition are men to be trusted with poisons and women not, unless that of their peculiar wickedness? While the spirit of the age and the tendency of all improvement is to make woman the equal of man, this Bill puts on them the stamp of the most degrading inferiority, precisely where the common voice of mankind proclaims them superior—in moral goodness.

If all the restrictions imposed by this Bill were common to men and women, it would be giving up, *pro tanto,* the peculiar and one of the most valuable characteristics of English freedom; it would be treating all mankind, except the Government and its agents, as children; but it would be giving an equal measure of justice to all, and would be no insult and disparagement peculiarly to any. The Legislature will not declare that Englishmen cannot be trusted with poisons, but it is not ashamed to assert that Englishwomen cannot. A law which, if common to both, would be merely a specimen of timidity and over-caution, is, when limited to women, a legislative declaration that Englishwomen are poisoners—Englishwomen as a class, as distinguished from Englishmen. And for what reason, or under what incitement, is this insult passed upon them? Because among the last dozen murders there were two or three cases, which attracted some public attention, of poisoning by women. Is it the part of a legislature to shape its laws to the accidental peculiarities of the latest crime reported in the newspapers? If the last two or three murderers had been men with red hair, as well might Parliament have rushed to pass an Act restricting all red-haired men from buying or possessing deadly weapons.

The silence of all who, from their position, could have made their voices heard, will, I hope, be my excuse for addressing to you, even at so late a period, this appeal.—I have the honour to be, Sir, your obedient servant,

J. S. MILL.

Progress and Education

As Mill grew older, increasing numbers of strangers consulted him about philosophical or social questions. Here is his answer to the Rev. H. W. Carr:[14]

7th January 1852.

SIR,—Want of time has prevented me from returning an earlier answer to your letter of 31st December. The question

[14] *Letters,* ed. Elliot, I, 165-67.

you ask me is one of the most difficult which any one can put either to others or to himself, namely, how to teach social science to the uneducated, when those who are called the educated have not learnt it; and nearly all the teaching given from authority is opposed to genuine morality.

What the poor as well as the rich require is not to be indoctrinated, is not to be taught other people's opinions, but to be induced and enabled to think for themselves. It is not physical science that will do this, even if they could learn it much more thoroughly than they are able to do. After reading, writing, and arithmetic (the last a most important discipline in habits of accuracy and precision, in which they are extremely deficient), the desirable thing for them seems to be the most miscellaneous information, and the most varied exercise of their faculties. They cannot read too much. Quantity is of more importance than quality, especially all reading which relates to human life and the ways of mankind; geography, voyages and travels, manners and customs, and romances, which must tend to awaken their imagination and give them some of the meaning of self-devotion and heroism, in short, to unbrutalise them. By such reading they would become, to a certain extent, cultivated beings, which they would not become by following out, even to the greatest length, physical science. As for education in the best sense of the term, I fear they have a long time to wait for it. The higher and middle classes cannot educate the working classes unless they are first educated themselves. The miserable pretence of education, which those classes now receive, does not form minds fit to undertake the guidance of other minds, or to exercise a beneficent influence over them by personal contact. Still, any person who sincerely desires whatever is for the good of all, however it may affect himself or his own class, and who regards the great social questions as matters of reason and discussion and not as settled long ago, may, I believe, do a certain amount of good by merely saying to the working classes whatever he sincerely thinks on the subjects on which they are interested. Free discussion with them as equals, in speech and in writing, seems the best instruction that can be given them, specially on social subjects.

With regard to the social question now before the public, and in which, as I gather from your letter, the working classes of your town have begun to take an interest, it seems to me chiefly important to impress on them—first, that they are quite right in aiming at a more equal distribution of wealth and social advantages; secondly, that this more equal distribution can only be permanently affected (for merely taking from Peter to give to Paul would leave things worse than even at present) by means of their own public spirit and self-devotion as regards others, and prudence and self-restraint in relation to themselves. At present their idea of social reform appears to be simply higher wages, and less work, for the sake of more sensual indulgence. To be independent of master manufacturers, to work for themselves and divide the whole produce of their labour is a worthy object of ambition, but it is only fit for, and can only succeed with people who can labour for the community of which they are a part with the same energy and zeal as if labouring for their own private and separate interest (the opposite is now the case), and who, instead of expecting immediately more pay and less work, are willing to submit to any privation until they have effected their emancipation. The French working men and women contended for a principle, for an idea of justice, and they lived on bread and water till they gained their purpose. It was not more and costlier eating and drinking that was their object, as it seems to be the sole object of most of the well-paid English artisans.

If in applying to me you hoped that I might be able to offer you any suggestions of more specific character, I hope you will attribute my not doing so to the difficulty of the subject and not to any want of will on my part.

[The following excerpts from a diary which Mill kept as an experiment in 1854 show the man considering both his own time and the future with his distinctive disinterested intelligence:[15]]

January 13. The inferiority of the present age is perhaps the consequence of its superiority. Scarcely any one, in the more educated classes, seems to have any opinions, or to place any real faith in those which he professes to have. At the same time, if we compare

---

[15] *Letters,* ed. Elliot, II, 359, 386.

the writings of any former period with those of the present, the superiority of these is unspeakable. We are astonished at the superficiality of the older writers; the little depths to which they sounded any question; the small portions of the considerations requiring to be looked at, which those writers appear to have seen. It requires in these times much more intellect to marshal so much greater a stock of ideas and observations. This has not yet been done, or has been done only by very few: and hence the multitude of thoughts only breeds increase of uncertainty. Those who should be the guides of the rest, see too many sides to every question. They hear so much said, or find that so much can be said, about everything, that they feel no assurance of the truth of anything. But where there are no strong opinions there are (unless, perhaps, in private matters) no strong feelings, nor strong characters.

April 13. In how many respects it is a changed world within the last half-dozen years. Free trade instead of restriction—cheap gold and cheapening, instead of dear and growing dearer—despotism (in France) instead of liberty—under-population instead of over-population—war instead of peace. Still, there is no real change in education, therefore all the other changes are superficial merely. It is still the same world. A slight change in education would make the world totally different.

April 14. The misfortune of having been born and being doomed to live in almost the infancy of human improvement, moral, intellectual, and even physical, can only be made less by the communion with those who are already what all well-organised human beings will one day be, and by the consciousness of oneself doing something, not altogether without value, towards helping on the slow but quickening progress towards that ultimate consummation.

April 15. The remedies for all our diseases will be discovered long after we are dead; and the world will be made a fit place to live in, after the death of most of those by whose exertions it will have been made so. It is to be hoped that those who live in those days will look back with sympathy to their known and unknown benefactors.

[Darwin's *On the Origin of Species* appeared at the end of 1859. Mill read it some months later, and found that he had to agree, at least to a considerable extent. Mill realized that Darwin was as deeply concerned with explaining change as he himself was.[16]]

11th April 1860.

. . . I have read since my return here several things which have interested me, above all Darwin's book. It far surpasses my expectation. Though he cannot be said to have proved the truth of his doctrine, he does seem to have proved that it *may* be true, which I take to be as great a triumph as knowledge and ingenuity could possibly achieve on such a question. Certainly nothing can be at first sight more entirely unplausible than his theory, and yet after beginning by thinking it impossible, one arrives at something like an actual belief in it, and one certainly does not relapse into complete disbelief. . . .

[Writing to an American, C. A. Cummings, Mill in 1863 supported proportional representation (the Hare system) as a solution to the problem on which he had worked for nearly forty years, the unequal distribution of education among the masses steadily being enfranchised:[17]]

. . . I do not, as you seem to think, take a gloomy view of human prospects. Few persons look forward to the future career of humanity with more brilliant hopes than I do. I see, however, many perils ahead, which unless successfully avoided would blast these prospects, and I am more specially in a position to give warning of them, since, being in strong sympathy with the general tendencies of which we are all feeling the effects, I am more likely to be listened to than those who may be suspected of disliking them. You think from American experience that I have overrated the magnitude of some of the dangers. I am, perhaps, of all Englishmen, the one who would most rejoice at finding that I had done so, and who most warmly welcomes every indication which favours such a conclusion. But whatever may be their amount, the dangers are real, and unless constantly kept in view, will tend to increase; and neither human nature nor experience justify the belief that mankind will be sufficiently on their guard against evils arising from their own shortcomings shared by those around them. In order that

---

[16] *Letters,* ed. Elliot, I, 236. The ellipsis points at the start of the letter appear in Elliot's text, and do not represent a deletion by the present editor.

[17] *Letters,* ed. Elliot, I, 289-90.

political principles, requiring the occasional sacrifice of immediate inclinations, should be habitually present to the minds of a whole people, it is generally indispensable that these principles should be embodied in institutions. I think it therefore essential that the principle that superior education is entitled to superior political might, should be in some way constitutionally recognised. I suggested plural voting as a mode of doing this: if there be any better mode I am ready to transfer my advocacy to that. But I attach far more importance to Mr. Hare's system of election, which it gives me the greatest pleasure to see you appreciate as I do. It would be worthy of America to inaugurate an improvement which is at once a more complete application than has ever been made of the democratic principle, and at the same time its greatest safeguard. With the system of representation of all instead of majorities only, and of the whole people instead of only the male sex, America would afford to the world the first example in history of true democratic equality. . . .

[In 1861 Mill wrote an essay on "The Subjection of Women." The theme led him to restate with great force some of the beliefs most important in his life.[18]]

. . . It is one of the characteristic prejudices of the reaction of the nineteenth century against the eighteenth, to accord to the unreasoning elements in human nature the infallibility which the eighteenth century is supposed to have ascribed to the reasoning elements. For the apotheosis of Reason we have substituted that of Instinct; and we call everything instinct which we find in ourselves and for which we cannot trace any rational foundation. This idolatry, infinitely more degrading than the other, and the most pernicious of the false worships of the present day, of all of which it is now the main support, will probably hold its ground until it gives way before a sound psychology laying bare the real root of much that is bowed down to as the intention of Nature and the ordinance of God. . . .

[18] *The Subjection of Women* (London: J. M. Dent & Sons, Ltd.; New York: E. P. Dutton & Co., 1929), pp. 221, 233-35, 239, 260-61. Reprinted by permission of J. M. Dent & Sons, Ltd., E. P. Dutton & Co. Inc., and Everyman's Library.

. . . What is the peculiar character of the modern world—the difference which chiefly distinguishes modern institutions, modern social ideas, modern life itself, from those of times long past? It is, that human beings are no longer born to their place in life, and chained down by an inexorable bond to the place they are born to, but are free to employ their faculties, and such favourable chances as offer, to achieve the lot which may appear to them most desirable. Human society of old was constituted on a very different principle. All were born to a fixed social position, and were mostly kept in it by law. . . . As some men are born white and others black, so some were born slaves and others freemen and citizens; some were born patricians, others plebeians; some were born feudal nobles, others commoners. . . . In modern Europe, and most in those parts of it which have participated most largely in all other modern improvements, diametrically opposite doctrines now prevail. Law and government do not undertake to prescribe by whom any social or industrial operation shall or shall not be conducted, or what modes of conducting them shall be lawful. These things are left to the unfettered choice of individuals. . . . The old theory was, that the least possible should be left to the choice of the individual agent; that all he had to do should, as far as practicable, be laid down for him by superior wisdom. Left to himself he was sure to go wrong. The modern conviction, the fruit of a thousand years of experience, is, that things in which the individual is the person directly interested, never go right but as they are left to his own discretion; and that any regulation of them by authority, except to protect the rights of others, is sure to be mischievous. . . . It is not that all processes are supposed to be equally good, or all persons to be equally qualified for everything; but that freedom of individual choice is now known to be the only thing which procures the adoption of the best processes, and throws each operation into the hands of those who are best qualified for it. Nobody thinks it necessary to make a law that only a strong-armed man shall be a blacksmith. Freedom and competition suffice to make blacksmiths strong-armed men, because the weak-armed can earn more by engaging in occupations for which they are more fit. . . .

If this general principle of social and economical science is not

true; if individuals, with such help as they can derive from the
opinion of those who know them, are not better judges than the
law and the government, of their own capacities and vocation;
the world cannot too soon abandon this principle, and return to
the old system of regulations and disabilities. But if the principle
is true, we ought to act as if we believed it, and not to ordain that
to be born a girl instead of a boy, any more than to be born black
instead of white, or a commoner instead of a nobleman, shall decide
the person's position through all life—shall interdict people from
all the more elevated social positions, and from all, except a few,
respectable occupations. . . .

Of all difficulties which impede the progress of thought, and
the formation of well-grounded opinions on life and social arrangements, the greatest is now the unspeakable ignorance and inatten-
tion of mankind in respect to the influences which form human
character. Whatever any portion of the human species now are, or
seem to be, such, it is supposed, they have a natural tendency
to be. . . . History, which is now so much better understood than
formerly, teaches another lesson: if only by showing the extraordinary susceptibility of human nature to external influences, and
the extreme variableness of those of its manifestations which are
supposed to be most universal and uniform. But in history, as in
travelling, men usually see only what they already had in their
own minds; and few learn much from history, who do not bring
much with them to its study. . . .

. . . To see the futurity of the species has always been the priv-
ilege of the intellectual élite, or of those who have learnt from
them; to have the feelings of that futurity has been the distinction,
and usually the martyrdom, of a still rarer élite. Institutions, books,
education, society, all go on training human beings for the old,
long after the new has come; much more when it is only coming.
But the true virtue of human beings is fitness to live together as
equals; claiming nothing for themselves but what they as freely
concede to everyone else; regarding command of any kind as an
exceptional necessity, and in all cases a temporary one; and pre-
ferring, whenever possible, the society of those with whom leading

and following can be alternate and reciprocal. To these virtues, nothing in life as at present constituted gives cultivation by exercise. The family is a school of despotism, in which the virtues of despotism, but also its vices, are largely nourished. Citizenship, in free countries, is partly a school of society in equality; but citizenship fills only a small place in modern life, and does not come near the daily habits or inmost sentiments. The family, justly constituted, would be the real school of the virtues of freedom. It is sure to be a sufficient one of everything else. . . . What is needed is, that it should be a school of sympathy in equality, of living together in love, without power on one side or obedience on the other. . . . The moral training of mankind will never be adapted to the conditions of the life for which all other human progress is a preparation, until they practise in the family the same moral rule which is adapted to the normal constitution of human society. Any sentiment of freedom which can exist in a man whose nearest and dearest intimacies are with those of whom he is absolute master, is not the genuine or Christian love of freedom, but, what the love of freedom generally was in the ancients and in the middle ages— an intense feeling of the dignity and importance of his own personality; making him disdain a yoke for himself, of which he has no abhorrence whatever in the abstract, but which he is abundantly ready to impose on others for his own interest or glorification.

KARL MARX

Marx believed that he had discovered the forces which really determined all change—in the past, in the tumultuous nineteenth century, in a future in which man's happiness would be assured by the relative changelessness of the world around him. Marx's conviction that he was absolutely right, and would be proved right for all eternity, partly explains the ferocity of his slashing style as a mature writer. That fierceness derives also from his awareness of the stubborn refusal of many intelligent and powerful people in his time to acknowledge the prime importance of change. Decorously qualified phrases would jolt no one; Marx bent his words, as he bent all of his labor, to the end that he might rock Europe to its foundations and thus demolish forever all pretense that the world had not changed or did not require any further changing.

Marx was born in 1818, into the family of a prospering Jewish lawyer in the Rhineland. His father had risen and was continuing to rise, economically, socially, and politically, by the energetic use of his talents in an environment becoming increasingly favorable to the use of such talents. The elder Marx decided that his own upward progress, and that of his family as well, would accelerate if they were converted to German Protestantism, and they were all baptized when Karl was six years old.

Taking advantage of the enlarged opportunities which conversion brought, the young Marx received an excellent education. When he was seventeen, he wrote an essay for a school examination which suggests that he treasured very great hopes. His expectation that he would live a life of considerable activity, and that that activity would have unmistakable importance, stands out sharply.[1]

[1] Edward L. Burke, S.J., "Karl Marx: Reflections of a Young Man on the Choice of a Career in Life," *The New Scholasticism*, XXXV (1961), 197, 201. The translation is Father Burke's. Reprinted by permission of *The New Scholasticism*.

Nature itself has determined the proper sphere of activity for the brute animal, and the animal peacefully perfects itself within that sphere without any attempt to go beyond it; without even suspecting that any other exists. The divinity has also given man a universal goal, the ennobling of himself and of mankind, but it has left it up to man himself to seek out the means by which he can attain it, he has left it up to him to choose within society that position which is most adapted to him and from which he can best benefit himself and society. . . .

History declares greatest those men who ennobled themselves by working for the common good; experience extols as happiest the man who has made the greatest number of men happy; and religion itself teaches us that the model which we all strive to imitate offered himself up for mankind, and who would dare to nullify such verdicts?

If we have chosen the profession where we can work best for mankind, then no burdens can overwhelm us because they are only sacrifices for all, then we enjoy no meagre, narrow, selfish joy, but our happiness belongs to millions, our actions live on silently but ever at work and our ashes are bedewed with the hot tears of noble men.

[Marx first studied law, and then history and philosophy, at the universities of Bonn and Berlin. He was convinced that he had been able to make his discoveries about the nature of change because his method of investigation proved superior to that used by any of his contemporaries. He always acknowledged his indebtedness for this achievement to the philosopher G. W. F. Hegel (1770-1831), whose work he pondered in his student days and long after. Hegel had striven mightily for an all-encompassing view of the process of change, which he called "dialectic." Hegel had seen correctly, Marx believed, that change took place as the result of struggle, and that the struggle must go on ceaselessly because causes gave rise to effects which then became causes of further effects. According to Marx, Hegel had not realized that this struggle pitted men against men as if they were animals: nothing more reasonable than an impersonal "law of population"—a function of the number of combatants—settled how much each man could snatch in the bestial struggle against those who supposedly were his fellow human beings.

Marx saw Hegel floating too far above the real, material world. He accepted Hegel's vision of a process of change which men could succeed in understanding, but insisted that the process was a struggle between very material, very tangible combatants. Marx described a central feature of his adult life, his materializing of Hegel's abstractly generalized view of change, in the preface (dated 1873) to the second edition of the first volume of *Das Kapital*. The following excerpts begin with Marx quoting a Russian article about his method in the book. He then explains that the essence of his method does not lie in any rejection of Hegel's basic pattern for understanding change, but rather in his reversal of the objects on which he would use Hegel's approach.[2]]

For Marx, only one thing is important: to discover the laws of the phenomena he is investigating. He is not interested only in the law which controls them in so far as they have a finished form and a mutual connexion within a definite historical period. He is still more interested in the law of their change, their evolution, that is to say the transition from one form to another, from one series of relations into a different one. As soon as he has discovered this law, he proceeds to work out in detail the effects as manifested in social life. . . . Consequently, Marx troubles himself about one thing only: to demonstrate, by means of exact scientific study, the necessity of definite and orderly successions in social relations, and, so far as possible, to give a perfectly correct statement of the facts which serve for the foundation and the support of his views. For this purpose, it is quite enough that, when demonstrating the necessity of the present order of society, he should simultaneously demonstrate the necessity of a different order into which the present order must inevitably pass, no matter whether human beings believe this or do not believe it, no matter whether they are aware of it or unaware of it. Marx regards the social movement as a natural process, guided by laws which are not merely independent of the will, the consciousness, and the purposes of men, but, conversely, determine their will, their consciousness, and their purposes. . . . If the conscious element plays a subordinate part in the history of civilisation, it is obvious that a critical enquiry whose subject matter is civilisation can, less than anything else, have for its basis any form or any result of consciousness. This means that the starting-point of the enquiry must be, not the idea, but only the external phenomenon. The criticism will confine itself to the comparison and confronting of a fact, not with an

---

[2] Marx, *Capital. A Critique of Political Economy. The Process of Capitalist Production,* trans. Eden and Cedar Paul (New York: International Publishers, 1929), pp. 871-74. The elisions in the quotation from the Russian are Marx's. Reprinted by permission of International Publishers Co., Inc., and George Allen & Unwin, Ltd.

idea, but with another fact. For this enquiry, what really matters is that both the facts shall be studied as accurately as possible; and that, as confronted with one another, they shall really constitute different evolutionary factors: and most important of all is it that there should be an accurate analysis of the sequences and the connexions out of which the stages of evolution are made up. But, we shall be told, the general laws of economic life are always one and the same, whether these laws are applied to the present or to the past. This is the very thing that Marx denies. According to him there are no such abstract laws. . . . In his opinion, every historical period has laws peculiar to itself. . . . As soon as life has passed through a given period of evolution, and is moving on from one stage to another, it begins to be subjected to the guidance of new laws. In a word, economic life goes through an evolutionary history resembling that with which we are familiar in other domains of biology. . . . The earlier economists misunderstood the nature of economic laws when they compared them with the laws of physics and chemistry. . . . A profounder analysis of the phenomena has shown that social organisms differ from one another as fundamentally as do vegetable and animal organisms. . . . Nay more, one and the same phenomenon is subject to quite different laws in different social organisms, because the general structure of these organisms differs, because their individual organs vary, because these organs function under different conditions, and so on. For instance, Marx denies that the law of population is the same at all times and in all places. He contends that every evolutionary phase has its own law of population. . . . As productivity develops, social conditions and the laws governing them change. Since it is Marx's aim to study and elucidate the capitalist economic order from this standpoint, he is satisfied to formulate in strictly scientific terms the purpose which every precise study of economic life must have. . . . The scientific value of such an investigation lies in the disclosure of the special laws that regulate the origin, existence, development, and death of a given social organism, and its replacement by another and a higher one. Such, in fact, is the value of Marx's book.

When the writer describes so aptly, and (so far as my personal application of it goes) so generously, the method I have actually used, what else is he describing but the dialectic method? . . .

My own dialectical method is not only fundamentally different from the Hegelian dialectical method, but is its direct opposite. For Hegel, the thought process (which he actually transforms into

an independent subject, giving to it the name of "idea") is the demiurge [creator] [3] of the real; and for him the real is only the outward manifestation of the idea. In my view, on the other hand, the ideal is nothing other than the material when it has been transposed and translated inside the human head.

Nearly thirty years ago, when Hegelianism was still fashionable, I criticised the mystifying aspect of the Hegelian dialectic. But at the very time when I was working at the first volume of *Das Kapital*, the peevish and arrogant mediocrities who nowadays have the ear of the educated public in Germany, were fond of treating Hegel much as in Lessing's day the world of Moses Mendelssohn used to treat Spinoza, namely as a "dead dog". That was why I frankly proclaimed myself a disciple of that great thinker, and even, in *Das Kapital*, toyed with the use of Hegelian terminology when discussing the theory of value. Although in Hegel's hands dialectic underwent a mystification, this does not obviate the fact that he was the first to expound the general forms of its movement in a comprehensive and fully conscious way. In Hegel's writings, dialectic stands on its head. You must turn it right way up again if you want to discover the rational kernel that is hidden away within the wrappings of mystification.

In its mystified form, dialectic became the fashion in Germany because it seemed to elucidate the existing state of affairs. In its rational form it is a scandal and an abomination to the bourgeoisie and its doctrinaire spokesmen, because, while supplying a positive understanding of the existing state of things, it at the same time furnishes an understanding of the negation of that state of things, and enables us to recognise that that state of things will inevitably break up; it is an abomination to them because it regards every historically developed social form as in fluid movement, as transient; because it lets nothing overawe it, but is in its very nature critical and revolutionary.

The contradictions inherent in the movement of capitalist society are most conspicuous to the practical bourgeois in the vicissitudes of the periodic cycles to which modern industry is subject, and in the culminating point of these cycles, a universal crisis. Such a crisis

[3] Translator's interpolation.

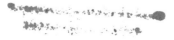

is once more approaching, although as yet in its preliminary stages. By its universality and its intensity, it will drum dialectics into the heads even of the upstarts of the New, Holy, Prussian-German Empire.

Alienation: Men Are Not Men

In Berlin the youthful Marx associated with younger followers of Hegel who had grown impatient with the master's acceptance of governmental restrictiveness, especially as manifested in Prussian rigidity. These disciples rejected Hegel's view of change as acceptable only as an object of theoretical inquiry, but never to be considered in any way that might lead to agitation for actual reform. Marx had intended to be a university teacher, but he found agreement with the view that the Prussian state had been everlastingly ordained to unchanging perfection a requirement which he could not meet. His views grew increasingly "radical," measured in terms of the monumental conservatism of the Prussian government, and finally a university career became impossible. Marx joined a newspaper staff and rose to be the paper's editor, but its advanced opinions resulted in its suppression at the start of 1843. In that year he married the daughter of a high government official, and the two prepared to face the hardships that had to follow rejecting safe and accepted positions.

Marx very early developed a desire to discover why change had affected him with such apparent cruelty and irreversibility. What had become of his father's hopes for a successful son? What forces had combined to cut him off from the fulfillment to which his education and his abilities entitled him? Must his adolescent desire for meaningful activity—and for ensuing fame—perish in bitter scrounging for bread to sustain an existence like that which was the lot of so many millions? His education and his feelings, both for himself and for others, led him to believe that many men were estranged from their own potential as really human beings: they were alienated from what they ought to be—creatures who truly were men.

No procedure could be more natural for someone so thoroughly steeped in Hegelian ways of thought than to see the problem as a struggle; no procedure could be more natural for one of Marx's age, experience, and temperament than to see the struggle as taking place between real, material opponents: a conflict between men striving to be men, and men determined to prevent the universal realization of what it meant to be a man. Marx had already heard and read something about socialism. Sensing that it might aid him powerfully in analyzing the history and present state of the struggle of men to be men, he now decided to make a thorough study of the large variety of socialist doctrines. He went to Paris, the great home of socialist thinkers. By the end of 1844 he had written a series of manuscripts, not published for nearly a century, in which he disclosed society's economic arrangements as the main device used to keep man a mere animal rather than a being conscious that he was a man and a member of a distinctive species, a mere mechanism rather than an individual aware of the typically human qualities which he shared with other men. Condemned to meager existence as they toiled for the benefit of employers, men were being deprived of the right to be men. They could lose nothing and would gain everything if they came to see how change had victimized them.[4]

The animal is one with its life activity. It does not distinguish the activity from itself. It is *its activity*. But man makes his life activity itself an object of his will and consciousness. He has a conscious life activity. It is not a determination with which he is completely identified. Conscious life activity distinguishes man from the life activity of animals. Only for this reason is he a species-being. Or rather, he is only a self-conscious being, i.e. his own life is an object for him, because he is a species-being. Only for this reason is his activity free activity. Alienated labour reverses the relationship, in that man because he is a self-conscious being makes his life activity, his *being*, only a means for his *existence*. . . .

[The more the worker produced, the less he possessed, and the more surely he fell under the sway of what he produced: capital. The worker himself produced the power to take away from himself what he produced above a scanty minimum needed to keep him existing: that power was capital. Only the worker could change the certainty that he would be kept as

[4] Marx, *Early Writings*, trans. T. B. Bottomore (New York: McGraw-Hill Book Company, Inc., 1964), pp. 127, 122-23, 120, 155. Reprinted by permission of McGraw-Hill Book Company, Inc., and C. A. Watts & Co., Ltd.

inhuman in the future as he was in the present. Orthodox political economy, such as the treatise which Mill published in 1848, confirmed the
desolateness of the prospect.]

All these consequences follow from the fact that the worker is
related to the *product of his labour* as to an *alien* object. For it is
clear on this presupposition that the more the worker expends
himself in work the more powerful becomes the world of objects
which he creates in face of himself, the poorer he becomes in his
inner life, and the less he belongs to himself. It is just the same as
in religion. The more of himself man attributes to God the less
he has left in himself. The worker puts his life into the object,
and his life then belongs no longer to himself but to the object.
The greater his activity, therefore, the less he possesses. What is
embodied in the product of his labour is no longer his own. The
greater this product is, therefore, the more he is diminished. The
alienation of the worker in his product means not only that his
labour becomes an object, assumes an *external* existence, but that
it exists independently, *outside himself*, and alien to him, and that
it stands opposed to him as an autonomous power. The life which
he has given to the object sets itself against him as an alien and
hostile force. . . .

We have begun from the presuppositions of political economy.
We have accepted its terminology and its laws. We presupposed
private property; the separation of labour, capital and land, as also
of wages, profit and rent; the division of labour; competition; the
concept of exchange value, etc. From political economy itself, in
its own words, we have shown that the worker sinks to the level of
a commodity, and to a most miserable commodity; that the misery
of the worker increases with the power and volume of his production; that the necessary result of competition is the accumulation
of capital in a few hands, and thus a restoration of monopoly in a
more terrible form; and finally that the distinction between capitalist and landlord, and between agricultural labourer and industrial worker, must disappear, and the whole of society divide into
the two classes of property *owners* and *propertyless* workers.

[Marx concluded that private property transformed men into victims and
sapped their capacity to be men. Seeking to change the degraded and

exploited into men, Marx turned to the type of socialism most outspokenly
committed to abolishing private property, and announced himself an
adherent of communism. The niceties and fine points of doctrinal definition mattered less at this time than Marx's utter conviction that all human problems would be solved if men could only be allowed to become
men.]

Communism is the *positive* abolition of *private property*, of
human self-alienation, and thus the real *appropriation* of *human*
nature through and for man. It is, therefore, the return of man
himself as a *social*, i.e. really human, being, a complete and conscious return which assimilates all the wealth of previous development. Communism as a fully developed naturalism is humanism
and as a fully developed humanism is naturalism. It is the *defini-
tive* resolution of the antagonism between man and nature, and
between man and man. It is the true solution of the conflict between existence and essence, between objectification and self-affir-
mation, between freedom and necessity, between individual and
species. It is the solution of the riddle of history and knows itself
to be this solution.

[Friedrich Engels (1820-1895) first visited Marx in 1844, and the close col-
laboration of the two began at once. Engels was the son of a German
industrialist, and worked as a factory manager, largely in England. Marx
came to rely on Engels as an extremely intelligent counterpart in his own
work both as theorist and agitator. Engels did not defer to Marx like an
uncritical automaton, but neither did he conceal his admiration for
Marx's genius.

The extraordinary duration and closeness of their association testifies to
their generosity with each other, a willingness to share that went far beyond Engels' financial rescue of Marx during some times of the most terrible impoverishment. In the later 1840s they were driven from Paris to
Brussels, back to France, then to Cologne, and again to Paris, constantly
agitating, propagandizing, attempting to organize the workers to use their
strength for change. All other social groups, they were convinced, had far
too important stakes in the avoidance of change. Marx and Engels finally
settled in London, the leading nineteenth-century refuge for radicals and
dissenters.

Marx's sense of the distance in his own life between expectation and
actuality led him, not to resignation or depression, but to a resilient determination which attracted many followers. The power of Marx's ana-

lytical mind and the zeal of his efforts for change bound his supporters to him. Wilhelm Liebknecht's reminiscence of his first meeting with Marx and Engels, in 1850, shows the impact Marx often had.[5]]

. . . The conversation gradually assumed a wider scope. Soon we were in the sphere of *natural science,* and Marx made fun of the victorious reaction in Europe, which imagined that it had stifled the revolution and did not suspect that natural science was preparing a new revolution. King Steam, who had revolutionized the world in the previous century, was coming to the end of his reign, and another, incomparably greater, revolutionist would take his place, the *electric spark.* And then Marx related to me, full of fire and enthusiasm, that for the last few days a model of an electric machine which pulled a railway train had been exhibited in Regent Street. "Now the problem has been solved—the consequences are unpredictable. The economic revolution must be followed by a political one, for the latter is only the expression of the former." Marx's conception of the world, and especially what later came to be termed the *materialist conception of history,* was so clearly expressed in the manner in which he discussed this progress of science and mechanics that certain doubts which I had hitherto entertained melted away like snow in the sunshine of spring. That evening I never went home at all—we spoke and joked and drank until late the next morning, and the sun was already high in the heavens when I went to bed. But not for long, I could not sleep. My head was too full of everything that I had heard. My thoughts, roving hither and thither, drove me out again and I hurried to Regent Street in order to see the model, this modern Trojan horse, which bourgeois society in suicidal fascination had introduced with rejoicing into their Ilion, as once the Trojan men and women had done with theirs, and which would bring about their certain destruction.

[Marx consistently refused to accept what had happened to him as his unalterable fate. Forced to abandon the life of fulfillment as a comfortably established bourgeois, for which his father and his own talents had destined him, he asked again and again: why did this happen to me? Why

[5] Marx and Engels, *Selected Works* (New York: International Publishers, n. d.), I, 104-5. Reprinted by permission of International Publishers Co., Inc.

must so many others suffer as I do, in mines and factories fit only for animals? How can I rouse them from their inhuman numbness?

Marx answered these questions in two major ways: by seeking to explain, through the analysis of the past, how men had been degraded into animals meant to toil until death finally ended their misery; and by seeking to bring his understanding of the past to those who suffered so that they would recognize that they had been enslaved, and then would act on the basis of their new knowledge. The changing of men into animals could be reversed if men grasped what had happened.

Those who toiled would have to save themselves, because no one else— except Marx and Engels—understood their plight enough to act effectively. Accordingly, Marx was ready to aid in efforts such as the attempt to revive Chartism, the most important mass movement in England for reform in the first half of the nineteenth century. Marx never agitated wildly; he always used his comprehension of the process of change as a guide in his organizational activity. Sentimental attacks on evil industrialists and emotional sketches of a paradisical future could never succeed, Marx believed, and he pointed to the record of failure which constituted the history of socialism.

In 1856 Marx was asked to give a toast, "for the sovereignty of the proletariat in all countries," at a banquet celebrating the anniversary of a Chartist paper. He responded with a speech strongly affirming his reliance on penetrating the realities which workers confronted, realities which the middle class sought to pass over quietly or "burke," realities about to be changed by the helpful sprite, Robin Goodfellow—symbolic of the aroused worker:[6]]

The so-called Revolutions of 1848 were but poor incidents— small fractures and fissures in the dry crust of European society. However, they denounced the abyss. Beneath the apparently solid surface, they betrayed oceans of liquid matter, only needing expansion to rend into fragments continents of hard rock. Noisily and confusedly they proclaimed the emancipation of the Proletarian, *i.e.*, the secret of the nineteenth century, and of the revolution of that century. That social revolution, it is true, was no novelty invented in 1848. Steam, electricity, and the self-acting mule were revolutionists of a rather more dangerous character than even citizens Barbès, Raspail and Blanqui. But, although the atmosphere in which we live, weighs upon every one with a 20,000 lb. force,

[6] Marx and Engels, *Sel. Works*, II, 427-29.

do you feel it? No more than European society before 1848 felt the revolutionary atmosphere enveloping and pressing it from all sides. There is one great fact, characteristic of this our nineteenth century, a fact which no party dares deny. On the one hand, there have started into life industrial and scientific forces, which no epoch of the former human history had ever suspected. On the other hand, there exist symptoms of decay, far surpassing the horrors recorded of the latter times of the Roman empire. In our days everything seems pregnant with its contrary. Machinery, gifted with the wonderful power of shortening and fructifying human labour, we behold starving and overworking it. The new-fangled sources of wealth, by some strange weird spell, are turned into sources of want. The victories of art seem bought by the loss of character. At the same pace that mankind masters nature, man seems to become enslaved to other men or to his own infamy. Even the pure light of science seems unable to shine but on the dark background of ignorance. All our invention and progress seem to result in endowing material forces with intellectual life, and in stultifying human life into a material force. This antagonism between modern industry and science on the one hand, modern misery and dissolution on the other hand; this antagonism between the productive powers, and the social relations of our epoch is a fact, palpable, overwhelming, and not to be controverted. Some parties may wail over it; others may wish to get rid of modern arts, in order to get rid of modern conflicts. Or they may imagine that so signal a progress in industry wants to be completed by as signal a regress in politics. On our part, we do not mistake the shape of the shrewd spirit that continues to mark all these contradictions. We know that to work well the new-fangled forces of society, they only want to be mastered by new-fangled men—and such are the working men. They are as much the invention of modern time as machinery itself. In the signs that bewilder the middle class, the aristocracy and the poor prophets of regression, we do recognise our brave friend, Robin Goodfellow, the old mole that can work in the earth so fast, that worthy pioneer—the Revolution. The English working men are the first born sons of modern industry. They will then, certainly, not be the last in aiding the social revolution produced by that industry, a revolution, which means the emancipation of their own class all over the world, which is as universal as capital-rule and wages-slavery. I know the heroic struggles the English working class have gone through since the middle of the last century—struggles less glorious, because they are shrouded in obscurity, and burked by the middle class historian. To revenge the misdeeds of the ruling class, there existed in the middle ages, in Germany, a secret tribunal, called the *"Vehmgericht."* If a red cross was seen marked on a house, people knew that its owner was doomed by the *"Vehm."* All the houses of Europe are now marked with the mysterious red cross. History is the judge —its executioner, the proletarian.

Science Will Explain Man's Condition

In 1857 a commercial crisis spurred Marx to resume his earlier studies of economics, and for some years he curtailed his practical efforts to organize the oppressed. He felt that he had to make a fresh start at understanding the nature of capitalism and the history of its development. He intended to examine capitalism as an economic system with corresponding political and social institutions more thoroughly than any investigator had ever treated it. More reliable knowledge could only speed the destruction of capitalism: workers who knew from reading Marx how capitalism had changed and had to continue changing would plan far more effective attacks.

The venture was too enormous: Marx never finished it, and in his lifetime only one volume of *Das Kapital* ever appeared. After his death an additional three volumes were quarried from surviving drafts and notes. In the 1860s Marx resumed actively plotting the downfall of capitalism, and his involvement in the International Working Men's Association cut sharply into the time and energy needed for theoretical work.

Marx wanted to probe capitalism scientifically. He shared the conviction of Mill and Spencer and many other Western thinkers about society: if a biologist or physicist could unravel natural processes and then use his knowledge to control them, so might the investigator of society, who would discover equally certain truths and apply them with similarly great expectations of success. Understanding past development—of a molecule, a hive of bees, a nation—assured control of the future. The workers would triumph because they had to, and their anticapitalist zeal would increase because they would understand Marx's demonstration that the future must belong to them. It is extremely characteristic of Marx to end the preface to the first edition (1867) of *Das Kapital*'s first volume by inviting "scientific criticism" and then reasserting his adherence to Dante's advice, "Follow your own bent, no matter what people say." Marx wanted to be a scientist, but he also wanted to be a leader of men, and in both roles he was serving a wish to triumph over forces that had deprived him of his destiny. Marx wanted to understand oppression and reaction, so that he might obliterate them. He worked as many of his contemporaries thought a scientist would, in order to reach a goal which a later generation would judge to be non-scientific. His devotion to a non-scientific purpose, however, does not eliminate the importance of his attempt to work scientifically. He derived extraordinary impetus from his conviction that at last someone would treat capitalism exactly as if it were an object for scientific scrutiny.[7]

The physicist pursues his investigations, either by studying natural processes where they manifest themselves in the most pregnant forms, and where they are obscured as little as possible by disturbing influences; or else, whenever he can, he performs experiments under conditions which ensure that the process he is watching shall run an uncomplicated course. The subject of study in the present work is the capitalist method of production, and the relations of production and exchange appropriate to that method. The region where these relations have hitherto assumed their most typical aspects, is England. That is why English conditions have been mainly drawn upon in illustration of my theoretical disquisitions. Should, however, the German reader be disposed to shrug his shoulders pharisaically when he contemplates the conditions under which the English industrial and agricultural workers live and perform their daily tasks, or if he should be inclined in optimistic mood to congratulate himself with the belief that things are far from being so bad in Germany, I must assure him: "De te fabula narratu." [The story is told about you; i.e., the cap fits.] [8]

---

[7] Marx, *Capital*, pp. 862-65. The English rendition of Dante's line is supplied by the translators.

[8] Translator's interpolation.

What we are concerned with primarily is, not the higher or the lower degree of development of the social antagonisms which arise out of the natural laws of capitalist production, but these laws in themselves, the tendencies which work out with an iron necessity towards an inevitable goal. A country in which industrial development is more advanced than in others, simply presents those others with a picture of their own future. . . .

Let us not deceive ourselves. Just as the American War of Independence in the eighteenth century sounded the tocsin for the middle classes of Europe, so the American Civil War in the nineteenth century has sounded the tocsin for the European working class. In England, the revolutionary process is plain to all who have eyes to see. When it reaches a certain intensity, it will necessarily react upon the Continent. There it will take a more brutal or a more humane form, according as the development of the working class itself varies. To say nothing of higher motives, the present ruling class will find it to its own interest to sweep away all the legally removable hindrances that interfere with the free development of the working class. That is one of the reasons why I have given so much space in the present work to a study of the history, the nature, and the results of British factory legislation. One nation can learn from others, and should do so. When a society has discovered the natural laws which regulate its own movement (and the final purpose of my book is to reveal the economic law of motion of modern society), it can neither overleap the natural phases of evolution, nor shuffle them out of the world by decrees. But this much, at least, it can do; it can shorten and lessen the birth-pangs.

One word more to avert misunderstandings. The persons of capitalists and landowners are not, in my book, depicted in rose-tinted colours; but if I speak of individuals, it is only in so far as they are personifications of economic categories, representatives of special class relations and class interests. Inasmuch as I conceive the development of the economic structure of society to be a natural process, I should be the last to hold the individual responsible for conditions whose creature he himself is, socially considered, however much he may raise himself above them subjectively.

In the domain of political economy, free scientific enquiry has its special enemies to encounter besides those who are met with on all other fields. The peculiar quality of its subject matter calls to arms against it the most violent, the most petty, and the most odious passions of the human heart—the furies of private interest. For instance, the Anglican Church will more readily pardon attacks upon thirty-eight of its thirty-nine articles, than upon one thirty-ninth of its income. To-day, even atheism is a venial sin as compared with the criticism of traditional property relations. Still, progress is undeniable. During the last few weeks there has been published a Blue Book entitled *Correspondence with Her Majesty's Missions Abroad regarding Industrial Questions and Trades' Unions*. The foreign representatives of the British crown tell us here, in plain words, that in Germany, France, in a word all the more advanced lands of the European continent, a change in the extant relations between capital and labour is just as obvious and just as inevitable as in England. Simultaneously there comes a voice from across the Atlantic, that of Mr. Wade, the vice-president of the United States of North America, who declares at public meetings that, after the abolition of slavery, a radical change in the conditions of capital and landed property comes next on the agenda! These are signs of the times, which can be hidden neither by purple mantles nor by black cassocks. They do not signify that miracles will happen to-morrow. Still, they do show that even the ruling classes are beginning to realise that contemporary society is not a solid crystal, but an organism capable of changing, and continually undergoing change.

The second volume of this work will deal with the circulation of capital (Book Two) and the varied forms assumed by capital in the general course of its development (Book Three). In a third and concluding volume (Book Four) I shall discuss the history of the theory.

I am ready to welcome scientific criticism. As far as concerns the prejudices of what is termed public opinion, to which I have never made any concessions, I shall continue to guide myself by the maxim of the great Florentine:

Sequi il tuo corso, e lascia dir le genti!

[Marx insisted that his work was scientific: he intended to demonstrate the universality of change through conflict. He saw his work as very much like Darwin's, and often referred to the English naturalist. At the end of 1860 he wrote to Engels:[9]]

During my time of trial, these last four weeks, I have read all sorts of things. Among others Darwin's book on Natural Selection. Although it is developed in the crude English style, this is the book which contains the basis in natural history for our view.

[Englishmen might understand something about change, but they could not describe it in the comprehensive, world-embracing fashion natural to one with many of the tastes of a Hegelian. Marx did like Darwin's destruction of supernatural purposes working themselves out in nature, as he wrote to Lassalle in 1861:[10]]

Darwin's book is very important and serves me as a basis in natural science for the class struggle in history. One has to put up with the crude English method of development, of course. Despite all deficiencies, not only is the death-blow dealt here for the first time to "teleology" in the natural sciences but their rational meaning is empirically explained.

[Marx saw Darwin as a kind of Marx:[11]]

Darwin has aroused our interest in the history of natural technology, that is to say in the origin of the organs of plants and animals as productive instruments utilised for the life purposes of these creatures.

[And at Marx's graveside, Engels saw him as a kind of Darwin:[12]]

Just as Darwin discovered the law of development of organic nature, so Marx discovered the law of the development of human history: the simple fact, hitherto concealed by an overgrowth of ideology, that mankind must first of all eat, drink, have shelter and clothing, before it can pursue politics, science, art, religion, etc.; that therefore the production of the immediate material means of subsistence and consequently the degree of economic development

[9] Marx and Engels, *Selected Correspondence 1846-1895*, trans. and ed. Dona Torr (New York: International Publishers, 1942), p. 126. Reprinted by permission of International Publishers Co., Inc. Marx's wife was ill.
[10] Marx and Engels, *Sel. Corr.*, p. 125.
[11] Marx, *Capital*, p. 392, n. 2.
[12] Marx and Engels, *Sel. Works*, I, 16.

attained by a given people or during a given epoch form the foundation upon which the state institutions, the legal conceptions, the ideas on art, and even on religion, of the people concerned have been evolved, and in the light of which they must, therefore, be explained, instead of *vice versa,* as had hitherto been the case. . . .

The Origins of Past and Present Misery

One of Engels' masterly summaries of his friend's major discoveries forms an excellent introduction to excerpts from *Das Kapital,* Marx's unfinished attempt to expound his understanding of change. In 1877 Engels described what Marx considered to be the roots in reality, the bases discoverable by a scientist, of socialism as a systematic attempt to undo past change.[13]

Of the many important discoveries through which Marx has inscribed his name in the annals of science, we can here dwell on only two.

The first is the revolution brought about by him in the whole conception of world history. The whole previous view of history was based on the conception that the ultimate causes of all historical changes are to be looked for in the changing ideas of human beings, and that of all historical changes political changes are the most important and are dominant in the whole of history. But the question was not asked as to whence the ideas come into men's minds and what the driving causes of the political changes are. Only upon the newer school of French, and partly also of English, historians had the conviction forced itself that, since the Middle Ages at least, the driving force in European history was the struggle of the developing bourgeoisie with the feudal aristocracy for social and political domination. Now Marx has proved that the whole of previous history is a history of class struggles, that in all the simple and complicated political struggles the only thing at issue has been the social and political rule of social classes, the maintenance of domination by older classes and the conquest of domination by newly arising classes. To what, however, do these

<hr/>

[13] Engels, "Karl Marx," in Marx and Engels, *Sel. Works,* I, 10-15.

classes owe their origin and their continued existence? They owe it to the particular material, physically sensible conditions in which society at a given period produces and exchanges its means of subsistence. The feudal rule of the Middle Ages rested on the self-sufficient economy of small peasant communities, which themselves produced almost all their requirements, in which there was almost no exchange and which received from the arms-bearing nobility protection from without and national or at least political cohesion. When the towns arose and with them separate handicraft industry and trade intercourse, at first internal and later international, the urban bourgeoisie developed, and already during the Middle Ages achieved, in struggle with the nobility, its inclusion in the feudal order as likewise a privileged estate. But with the discovery of the extra-European world, from the middle of the fifteenth century onwards, this bourgeoisie acquired a far more extensive sphere of trade and therewith a new spur for its industry; in the most important branches handicrafts were supplanted by manufacture, now on a factory scale, and this again was supplanted by large-scale industry, become possible owing to the discoveries of the previous century, especially that of the steam engine. Large-scale industry, in its turn, reacted on trade by driving out the old manual labour in backward countries, and creating the present-day new means of communication: steam engines, railways, electric telegraphy, in the more developed ones. Thus the bourgeoisie came more and more to combine social wealth and social power in its hands, while it still for a long period remained excluded from political power, which was in the hands of the nobility and the monarchy supported by the nobility. But at a certain stage—in France since the Great Revolution—it also conquered political power, and now in turn became the ruling class over the proletariat and small peasants. From this point of view all the historical phenomena are explicable in the simplest possible way—with sufficient knowledge of the particular economic condition of society, which it is true is totally lacking in our professional historians, and in the same way the conceptions and ideas of each historical period are most simply to be explained from the economic conditions of life and from the social and political relations of the period, which are in turn determined by these economic conditions. History was for the first time placed on its real basis; the palpable but previously totally over-looked fact that men must first of all eat, drink, have shelter and clothing, therefore must *work*, before they can fight for domination, pursue politics, religion, philosophy, etc.—this palpable fact at last came into its historical rights.

This new conception of history, however, was of supreme signifi-cance for the socialist outlook. It showed that all previous history moved in class antagonisms and class struggles, that there have always existed ruling and ruled, exploiting and exploited classes, and that the great majority of mankind has always been condemned to arduous labour and little enjoyment. Why is this? Simply because in all earlier stages of development of mankind production was so little developed that the historical development could proceed only in this antagonistic form, that historical progress as a whole was assigned to the activity of a small privileged minority, while the great mass remained condemned to producing by their labour their own meagre means of subsistence and also the increasingly rich means of the privileged. But the same investigation of history, which in this way provides a natural and reasonable explanation of the previous class rule, otherwise only explicable from the wickedness of man, also leads to the realization that, in consequence of the so tremendously increased productive forces of the present time, even the last pretext has vanished for a division of mankind into rulers and ruled, exploiters and exploited, at least in the most advanced countries; that the ruling big bourgeoisie has fulfilled its historic mission, that it is no longer capable of the leadership of society and has even become a hindrance to the development of production, as the trade crises, and especially the last great collapse, and the depressed condition of industry in all countries have proved; that historical leadership has passed to the proletariat, a class which, owing to its whole position in society, can only free itself by abolishing altogether all class rule, all servitude and all exploitation; and that the social productive forces, which have out-grown the control of the bourgeoisie, are only waiting for the asso-ciated proletariat to take possession of them in order to bring about a state of things in which every member of society will be enabled to participate not only in production but also in the distribution and administration of social wealth, and which so increases the social productive forces and their yield by planned operation of the whole of production that the satisfaction of all reasonable needs will be assured to everyone in an ever-increasing measure.

The second important discovery of Marx is the final elucidation of the relation between capital and labour, in other words, the demonstration how, within present society and under the existing capitalist mode of production, the exploitation of the worker by the capitalist takes place. Ever since political economy had put forward the proposition that labour is the source of all wealth and of all value, the question became inevitable: How is this then to be reconciled with the fact that the wageworker does not receive the whole sum of value created by his labour but has to surrender a part of it to the capitalist? Both the bourgeois economists and the Socialists exerted themselves to give a scientifically valid answer to this question, but in vain, until at last Marx came forward with the solution. This solution is as follows: The present-day capitalist mode of production presupposes the existence of two social classes —on the one hand, that of the capitalists, who are in possession of the means of production and subsistence, and, on the other hand, that of the proletarians, who, being excluded from this possession, have only a single commodity for sale, their labour power, and who therefore have to sell this labour power of theirs in order to obtain possession of means of subsistence. The value of a commodity is, however, determined by the socially necessary quantity of labour embodied in its production, and, therefore, also in its reproduction; the value of the labour power of an average human being during a day, month or year is determined, therefore, by the quantity of labour embodied in the quantity of means of subsistence necessary for the maintenance of this labour power during a day, month or year. Let us assume that the means of subsistence of a worker for one day require six hours of labour for their production, or, what is the same thing, that the labour contained in them represents a quantity of labour of six hours; then the value of labour power for one day will be expressed in a sum of money which also em- bodies six hours of labour. Let us assume further that the capitalist who employs our worker pays him this sum in return, pays him, therefore, the full value of his labour power. If now the worker works six hours of the day for the capitalist, he has completely replaced the latter's outlay—six hours' labour for six hours' labour. But then there would be nothing in it for the capitalist, and the latter therefore looks at the matter quite differently. He says: I have bought the labour power of this worker not for six hours but for a whole day, and accordingly he makes the worker work 8, 10, 12, 14 or more hours, according to circumstances, so that the product of the seventh, eighth and following hours is a product of unpaid labour and wanders, to begin with, into the pocket of the capitalist. Thus the worker in the service of the capitalist not only reproduces the value of his labour power, for which he receives pay, but over and above that he also produces a *surplus value* which, appropriated in the first place by the capitalist, is in its further course divided according to definite economic laws among the whole capitalist class and forms the basic stock from which arise ground rent, profit, accumulation of capital, in short, all the wealth consumed or accumulated by the non-labouring classes. But this proved that the acquisition of riches by the present-day capitalists consists just as much in the appropriation of the unpaid labour of others as that of the slave owner or the feudal lord exploiting serf labour, and that all these forms of exploitation are only to be distinguished by the difference in manner and method by which the unpaid labour is appropriated. This, however, also removed the last justification for all the hypocritical phrases of the possessing classes to the effect that in the present social order right and justice, equality of rights and duties and a general harmony of interests prevail, and present-day bourgeois society, no less than its predecessors, was exposed as a grandiose institution for the exploitation of the huge majority of the people by a small, ever-diminishing minority.

Modern, scientific Socialism is based on these two important facts. . . .

[Marx had found the origin of the entire sequence of changes which kept most men subhuman. The bite of his style and the title of the section from *Das Kapital* which follows show the involvement of both the dispassionate inquirer and the impassioned renovator in uncovering the "Secret of Primary Accumulation:" [14]]

We have seen how money is transformed into capital; how by means of capital, surplus value is made, and how out of surplus

[14] Marx, *Capital*, pp. 790-92.

value, more capital is made. But the accumulation of capital presupposes surplus value; surplus value presupposes capitalist production; capitalist production presupposes the existence of considerable quantities of capital and labour power in the hands of the producers of commodities. The whole movement, therefore, seems to turn in a vicious circle, out of which we can only make our way by the assumption that, as a prelude to capitalist accumulation, there has been a process of primary accumulation (Adam Smith terms it "previous accumulation")—an accumulation which is not the outcome of the capitalist method of production, but the starting-point thereof.

In political economy, this primary accumulation plays much the same part that is played by original sin in theology. Sin came into the world because Adam ate the forbidden fruit. The origin of sin is supposed to be explained by a folk-tale. In like manner we are told, as regards primary accumulation, that in times long past there were two sorts of people: some of them, the chosen few, were industrious, intelligent, and, above all, thrifty; the others, lazy rascals, wasted their substance in riotous living. But there is a difference. The theological legend of the Fall tells us this much, at least, why man has been condemned to eat his bread in the sweat of his face. On the other hand, the economic history of the Fall reveals to us why there are persons who need do nothing of the kind. No matter! It is from this economic Fall that dates the poverty of the masses, who, for all time, however hard they may work, have nothing to sell but themselves; and thence, likewise, dates the wealth of the few, which continually grows, although the few have long since ceased to work. People still chew the cud of this childish imbecility. Monsieur Thiers, for instance, retails it with statesmanlike solemnity in defence of property, retails it to his compatriots, at one time a talented nation. As soon as the question of property crops up, it becomes a sacred duty to declare that the spelling book should be the only reading of persons of all ages and all stages of mental development. In the history of the real world, as every one knows, conquest, subjugation, robbery, murder —in a word, force—play leading roles. But the gentle science of political economy has always clung to idyllic notions. "Right and labour", say the economists, have ever been the sole means of enrichment, "our own times" alone excepted. As a matter of fact, the methods of primary accumulation were anything but idyllic!

Money and commodities are not, from the first, capital, any more than the means of production and the means of subsistence are. They have to be transformed into capital. But this transformation can only take place under definite conditions, of which the following form the essentials. Two very different kinds of commodity owners must confront one another and enter into a mutual relation. On the one hand, there must be the owners of money, of the means of production, and of the means of subsistence, who desire by the purchase of others' labour power, to increase the sum of the values they own. On the other hand, there must be free workers, the sellers of their own labour power, and therefore the sellers of labour. They must be "free" workers in a double sense. First of all, they must not themselves form a direct part of the means of production, must not belong to the means of production, as do slaves, serfs, etc. Secondly, the means of production must not belong to them, as the means of production belong to peasant proprietors. Free workers are free from, unencumbered by, any means of production of their own. With this polarisation of the commodity market, the fundamental conditions requisite for capitalist production exist. The capitalist system presupposes a divorce between the workers and the ownership of the property through which alone their labour can become effective. As soon as capitalist production is able to stand on its own feet, it does not merely receive this divorce between labour and the means of labour as a legacy from the past, but reproduces it upon a continually increasing scale. The process which clears the way for the capitalist system, therefore, can be nothing else than the process whereby the worker is divorced from ownership of the means of labour; a process which, on the one hand, transforms the social means of subsistence and the social means of production into capital; and, on the other, transforms the actual producers into wage workers. The so-called primary accumulation, therefore, is nothing other than the historical process whereby the producer is divorced from the means of production. It assumes a "primary" aspect because it belongs to the primary phase that is traversed immediately before the history of capitalism begins, immediately before the establishment of the method of production proper to capitalism. . . .

[Marx wanted to create a panoramic view of the factory system and to compel belief by the pressure of the evidence which he found so abundantly. If he could do what Darwin had done, the workers would listen, and the owning classes would pay attention. He could not, however, describe the changing of men into animals and keep his writing untouched by his outraged feelings, for their fate reminded him of his own. In redeeming them he would bring redemption to the enslaved and despised of past ages and of future centuries, and to himself.[15]]

One who has to work at a machine, has to be trained to it from early youth upwards, so that he can learn to adapt his own movements to the uniform and continuous motion of an automaton. In so far as the machinery as a whole forms a system of manifold machines, working simultaneously and in concert, the cooperation based upon the use of machinery requires the distribution of differing groups of workers among the different machines. But machinofacture does away with the need for stereotyping this distribution, as it is stereotyped in the manufacturing system, by the persistent annexation of a particular man to a particular function. Since the integral movement of the factory does not proceed from the worker but from the machine, there can be a continuous change of personnel without any interruption of the labour process. The most striking proof of this is afforded by the relay system which was put into operation by the British factory owners during their revolt from 1848 to 1850. Finally, the quickness with which young people can learn to work at a machine, is another reason why it is necessary to train up a special class of workers who will function exclusively as machine operatives. As regards the work of the mere hodmen, this can, to some extent, be replaced in the mills by machines,[16] and, owing to its great simplicity, no difficulty attaches to

[15] Marx, *Capital*, pp. 449-56. The following footnotes, to n. 21, are Marx's; some of his other notes in this selection have been omitted, but his text has not been cut.

[16] Here is an example. Since the Act of 1844 was passed, various mechanical appliances have been introduced into woollen mills in order to replace the labour of children. When the children of the quality, the children of the factory owners themselves, have to go through a course of schooling as helpers in the

a rapid and constant change in the individuals burdened with this drudgery.

Although, then, machinery makes an end, technically speaking, of the old system of the division of labour, that system lingers for a time in the factory, as a custom handed down from manufacture, and is subsequently remoulded systematically, and established in a yet more hideous form as a means for the exploitation of labour power. The life-long specialty of handling the same tool which performs a partial operation, becomes the life-long specialty for serving a machine which performs a partial operation. Machinery is misused, in order to transform the worker from childhood upwards into part of a detail machine. In this way, not only are the expenses of the worker's reproduction considerably lessened, but at the same time his absolute dependence upon the factory as a whole (upon the capitalist, that is to say) is perfected. Here, as everywhere, we must distinguish between the greater productivity which is due to the development of the social process of production, and the greater productivity which is due to the capitalist exploitation of that process.

In manufacture and in handicrafts, the worker uses a tool; in the factory, he serves a machine. In the former case, the movements of the instrument of labour proceed from the worker; but in the latter, the movements of the worker are subordinate to those of the machine. In manufacture, the workers are parts of a living mechanism. In the factory, there exists a lifeless mechanism independent of them, and they are incorporated into that mechanism as its living appendages. "The dull routine of ceaseless drudgery and toil, in which the same mechanical process is incessantly repeated, resembles the torment of Sisyphus—the toil, like the rock,

---

factory, this almost unexplored domain of mechanics will be characterised by remarkable progress. "Of machinery, perhaps self-acting mules are as dangerous as any other kind. Most of the accidents from them happen to little children, from their creeping under the mules to sweep the floor while the mules are in motion. Several 'minders' have been fined for this offence, but without much general benefit. If machine makers would only invent a self-sweeper by whose use the necessity for these little children to creep under the machinery might be prevented, it would be a happy addition to our protective measures." *Reports of Inspectors of Factories,* October 31, 1866, p. 63.

recoils perpetually upon the wearied operative."[17] While labour at the machine has a most depressing effect upon the nervous system, it at the same time hinders the multiform activity of the muscles, and prohibits free bodily and mental activity. Even the lightening of the labour becomes a means of torture, for the machine does not free the worker from his work, but merely deprives his work of interest. All kinds of capitalist production, in so far as they are not merely labour processes, but also processes for promoting the self-expansion of capital, have this in common, that in them the worker does not use the instruments of labour, but the instruments of labour use the worker. However, it is only in machine production that this inversion acquires a technical and palpable reality. Through its conversion into an automaton, the instrument of labour comes to confront the worker during the labour process as capital, as dead labour, which controls the living labour power and sucks it dry. The divorce of the intellectual powers of the process of production from the manual labour, and the transformation of these powers into powers of capital over labour, are completed (as previously indicated) in large-scale industry based upon machine production. The special skill of each individual machine worker who is thus sucked dry, dwindles into an insignificant item as contrasted with the science, with the gigantic forces of nature, and with the mass of social labour, which are incorporated into the machine system, and out of which the power of the "master" is made. This master, in whose brain the machinery and his monopoly of it are inseparably intertwined, tells his "hands" contemptuously whenever he is at odds with them: "The factory operatives should keep in wholesome remembrance the fact that theirs is really a low species of skilled labour; and that there is none which is more easily acquired, or of its quality more amply remunerated,

---

[17] J. P. Kay, M.D., *The Moral and Physical Conditions of the Working Classes*, etc., 1832, p. 8.—Even an ordinary and optimistic free trader, Monsieur Molinari, remarks: "A man becomes worn out more quickly when supervising for fifteen hours a day the uniform movements of a mechanism than by exercising his own physical energies for the same space of time. This work of supervision, which would perhaps be useful training for the intelligence if it were not unduly prolonged, destroys in the long run, through its excess, mind and body alike." G. de Molinari, *Études économiques*, Paris, 1846.

or which by a short training of the least expert can be more quickly, as well as more abundantly acquired. . . . The master's machinery really plays a far more important part in the business of production than the labour and the skill of the operative, which six months' education can teach, and a common labourer can learn." [18]

The technical subordination of the worker to the uniform movement of the instrument of labour, and the peculiar composition of the working body (which is made up of individuals of both sexes and various ages), give rise to a barrack-like discipline, which is elaborated into a complete factory system, involving a full development of the previously described work of supervision—this meaning the division of the workers into operatives and overlookers, into the private soldiers and the non-commissioned officers of an industrial army. "The main difficulty [in the automatic factory] . . . lay . . . above all in training human beings to renounce their desultory habits of work, and to identify themselves with the unvarying regularity of the complex automaton. To devise and administer a successful code of factory discipline, suited to the necessities of factory diligence, was the Herculean enterprise, the noble achievement, of Arkwright! Even at the present day, when the system is perfectly organised and its labour lightened to the utmost, it is found nearly impossible to convert persons past the age of puberty into useful factory hands." [18] The factory code (in which capital formulates its autocracy over its workers—in a private legislative system, and without the partition of authority and the representative methods which in other fields are so much loved by the bourgeoisie) is only the capitalist caricature of that social regulation of the labour process which becomes necessary when cooperation is undertaken upon a large scale and when joint instruments of labour in the form of machinery are set to work. In place of the slave driver's lash, we have the overlooker's book of

[18] *The Master Spinners' and Manufacturers' Defence Fund, Report of the Committee,* Manchester, 1854, p. 17.

[19] [Marx cites here a Scotch writer on economics, Andrew Ure.]—No one who knows the life-story of Arkwright will be inclined to apply the epithet "noble" to this talented barber. Of all the great inventors of the eighteenth century, he was beyond question the arch-thief as far as other people's inventions were concerned, and a fellow of the basest sort.

penalties. Of course, all the punishments take the form of fines and deductions from wages; and the legislative talent of the factory Lycurgus is utilised in such a way that, as far as possible, a breach of the regulations is made even more profitable to the employer than their strict observance.[19]

[20] "Nowhere is the slavery imposed by the bourgeoisie upon the proletariat so glaringly manifest as in the factory. Here, both legally and in actual fact, freedom is at an end. The worker must be at the factory by half-past five in the morning. Should he come a minute or two late, he is fined; should he be ten minutes late, he is not admitted until breakfast is over, and he thus loses a quarter of a day's wages. He must eat, drink, and sleep, at the word of command. . . . The despotic whistle summons him from his bed, calls him away from his breakfast and his dinner. And what happens, once he is inside the factory? There, the factory owner is an absolute legislator. He issues factory regulations according to his own sweet will and pleasure; he alters his code and makes additions to it just as he likes; and even if he issues the most absurd regulations, the courts say to the worker: 'Since you entered into this contract of your own free will, you must abide by it.' . . . These workers are sentenced to life under the rod (both actually and metaphorically) from the age of nine until the day of their death." [Marx here cites a work by Engels.]—Let me give two examples of what "the courts say". One of them comes from Sheffield, towards the end of the year 1866. A workman had signed on for two years at a steel works in that town. Having had a quarrel with the owner, he left the works declaring, that in no circumstances would he work for that master any more. He was prosecuted for breach of contract, and was sentenced to two months' imprisonment. (If the master breaks the contract, he can only be sued in a civil court, and he risks nothing worse than a fine.) When the workman had served his two months' imprisonment, the owner invited him to return to the works in accordance with the terms of the old contract. The workman refused. He had already been punished for the breach of contract. The owner prosecuted him once more, and the court renewed its sentence, although one of the judges, Mr. Shee, publicly declared it to be a legal monstrosity that a man could be periodically punished for one and the same offence or crime throughout his life-time. This judgment was not given by the "Great Unpaid", the provincial Dogberries, but by the judges of one of the highest courts of justice in London.—[Note by Engels to the fourth German edition: This has now been abolished. Except in a few instances, such as public gasworks, the English worker has been placed on the same footing as his employer as regards breach of contract, and can only be sued in the civil courts.]—The second case comes from Wiltshire, at the end of November 1863. About thirty power-loom weavers in the employ of one Harrupp, a clothmaker at Leower's Mill, Westbury Leigh, went on strike because of Harrupp's pleasant little way of making deductions from their wages when they were late in the morning: 6d. for two minutes; 1s. for three minutes; and 1s. 6d. for ten minutes. This is at the rate of 9s. per hour, and £4 10s. per day; while the wages of the weavers never exceed, on the average, 10s. to 12s. a week. Harrupp also engaged a boy to announce the starting-time by a whistle, which the youngster often did before 6 o'clock in the morning. If the hands were not all there directly the whistle stopped blowing, the doors were closed, and those

We shall here be content to make passing allusion to the material conditions under which factory work is carried on. All the sense organs are alike injured by the artificially raised temperature, by the contamination of the air with fragments of the raw material, by the deafening noise, etc., etc.—to say nothing of the danger to life and limb that results from the close packing of the machinery, which, with the regularity of the seasons, fills its lists of those killed and wounded in the industrial process. Economy of the social means of production, which is not pursued by forcing-house methods until the factory system comes into operation, is, in the hands of capital, furthermore, a means for the systematic spoliation of the worker's vital necessaries while he is engaged at his work. He is robbed of space, of air, of light, and of protection of his

---

hands who were outside were fined. Since there were no clocks in the building, the unhappy hands were wholly at the mercy of the young timekeeper, who was inspired by Mr. Harrupp. The hands on strike, matrons and girls, declared that they were willing to go to work again if the timekeeper were replaced by a clock, and a more reasonable tariff of fines were introduced. Harrupp summoned nineteen women and girls before the magistrates for breach of contract. Each of them was sentenced to 6d. fine and 2s. 6d. costs, much to the indignation of all those members of the public who were present in the court. Harrupp was followed from the court by a crowd of people who hooted him.—A favourite occupation with factory owners is to punish the workers by imposing fines on them because of defects in the materials worked on. In 1866, this method led to a general strike in the English potteries. The *Reports of the Children's Employment Commission* (1863-1866) mention cases in which the worker, instead of receiving any wages for his work, was left, thanks to the imposition of fines, in debt to his worthy master. The recent cotton crisis furnished edifying examples of the skill displayed by these factory autocrats in making deductions from wages. Mr. R. Baker, inspector of factories, writes: "I have myself had lately to direct prosecutions against one cotton-mill occupier for having in these pinched and painful times deducted 10d. a piece from some of the young workers employed by him for the surgeon's certificate (for which he himself had only paid 6d.) when only allowed by the law to deduct 3d. and by custom nothing at all. . . . And I have been informed of another, who, in order to keep without the law, but to attain the same object, charges the poor children who work for him a shilling each, as a fee for learning them the art and mystery of cotton spinning, so soon as they are declared by the surgeon fit and proper persons for that occupation. There may therefore be undercurrent causes for such extraordinary exhibitions as strikes, not only whatever they arise, but particularly at such times as the present, which, without explanation, render them inexplicable to the public understanding." Mr. Baker is alluding here to a strike of power-loom weavers at Darwen, June 1863. See *Reports of Inspectors of Factories*, April 30, 1863, pp. 50-51.—The reader should note that these reports always overlap their official dates.

person against the dangerous and unwholesome accompaniments of the productive process—to say nothing of the way in which he is robbed of appliances for comfort while he is at work.[20] Was Fourier wrong when he spoke of a factory as "a mitigated form of convict prison"?

The Inevitable Future

Marx came up against the same difficulty which confronted all nineteenth-century investigators of change: an understanding of past sequences of change could never guarantee that future sequences would prove comprehensible, and hence alterable. Yet Marx could not yield to a mere inexorability of logic. His compassion for the distress of his age led him to hope that change would continue as he had grasped it, and would accelerate. The future would have to be made possible by the "Historical Tendency of Capitalist Accumulation." [21]

What does the primary accumulation of capital, its historical origin, amount to? In so far as it is not the direct transformation of slaves and serfs into wage earners (a mere change of form), it signifies nothing other than the expropriation of the immediate producers, that is to say the making an end of private property based upon the labour of its owner.

Private property, as contrasted with social or collective property,

[21] In the first part of Book Three, I shall give an account of a recent campaign on the part of the English factory owners against the clauses of the Factory Acts that aim at protecting the "hands" against dangerous machinery. Enough here to quote from the official report of Factory Inspector Leonard Horner: "I have heard some mill owners speak with inexcusable levity of some of the accidents; such, for instance, as the loss of a finger, being a trifling matter. A working man's living and prospects depend so much upon his fingers, that any loss of them is a very serious matter to him. When I have heard such inconsiderate remarks made, I have usually put this question: 'Suppose you were in want of an additional workman and two were to apply, both equally well qualified in other respects, but one had lost a thumb or a forefinger, which would you engage?' There never was a hesitation as to the answer." The manufacturers have "mistaken prejudices against what they have heard represented as a pseudo-philanthropic legislation". Reports of Inspectors of Factories, October 31, 1855.—These factory owners are clever fellows, and they certainly had good reason for their enthusiastic support of the slave-holder's rebellion!

[22] Marx, Capital, pp. 844-47. Two notes by Marx have been omitted.

exists only where the means of labour and the external conditions of labour belong to private individuals. But the character of private property differs according as the private individuals are workers or non-workers. The innumerable shades which, at the first glance, seem to be exhibited by private property, are merely reflexions of the intermediate conditions that lie between these two extremes.

The worker's private ownership of the means of production is the basis of petty industry; and petty industry is an indispensable condition for the development of social production and of the free individuality of the worker. Of course, this method of production is also found within the slaveholding system, within the system of serfdom, and within other dependent relationships. But it only flourishes, only manifests its full energy, only assumes its adequate and classical form, where the worker is the free private owner of the means of labour which he uses; only when the peasant owns the land he tills, and when the handicraftsman owns the tools which he handles as a virtuoso.

This method of production presupposes a parcelling-out of the soil, a scattered ownership of the instruments of production. Just as it excludes concentration of these means into a few hands, so does it exclude cooperation, the division of labour within the process of production, the social mastery and regulation of the forces of nature, the free development of the social energies of production. It is only compatible with narrow limits for production and society, limits that are the outcome of spontaneous growth. The desire to perpetuate the existence of such limits would be, as Pecqueur has rightly said: "a decree for the perpetuation of universal mediocrity". At a certain level of development, this method of production brings into the world material means which will effect its own destruction. Thenceforward there stir within the womb of society forces and passions which feel this method of production to be a fetter. It must be destroyed, it is destroyed. Its destruction, the transformation of the individual and scattered means of production into socially concentrated means of production, the transformation of the pygmy property of the many into the titan property of the few, the expropriation of the great masses of the people from the land, from the means of subsistence, and from the instruments of labour—this terrible and grievous expropriation of the populace—comprises the prelude to the history of capital. It comprises a series of forcible measures, of which we have passed in review those only that have been epoch-making as methods of the primary accumulation of capital. The expropriation of the immediate producers is effected with ruthless vandalism; and under the stimulus of the most infamous, the basest, the meanest, and the most odious of passions. Self-earned private property, the private property that may be looked upon as grounded on a coalescence of the isolated, individual, and independent worker, with his working conditions, is supplanted by capitalist private property, which is maintained by the exploitation of others' labour, but of labour which, in a formal sense, is free.

As soon as this process of transformation has sufficiently disintegrated the old society, has decomposed it through and through; as soon as the workers have been metamorphosed into proletarians, and their working conditions into capital; as soon as the capitalist method of production can stand upon its own feet—then the further socialisation of labour and the further transformation of the land and of the other means of production into socially utilised (that is to say, communal) means of production, which implies the further expropriation of private owners, takes on a new form. What has now to be expropriated, is no longer the labourer working on his own account, but the capitalist who exploits many labourers.

This expropriation is brought about by the operation of the immanent laws of capitalist production, by the centralisation of capital. One capitalist lays a number of his fellow capitalists low. Hand-in-hand with such centralisation, concomitantly with the expropriation of many capitalists by a few, the cooperative form of the labour process develops to an ever increasing degree; therewith we find a growing tendency towards the purposive application of science to the improvement of technique; the land is more methodically cultivated; the instruments of labour tend to assume forms which are only utilisable by combined effort; the means of production are economised through being turned to account only by joint, by social labour. All the peoples of the world are enmeshed in the net of the world market, and therefore the capitalist regime tends more and more to assume an international character. While there is thus a progressive diminution in the number of the capitalist magnates (who usurp and monopolise all the advantages of this transformative process), there occurs a corresponding increase in the mass of poverty, oppression, enslavement, degeneration, and exploitation; but at the same time there is a steady intensification of the wrath of the working class—a class which grows ever more numerous, and is disciplined, unified, and organised by the very mechanism of the capitalist method of production. Capitalist monopoly becomes a fetter upon the method of production which has flourished with it and under it. The centralisation of the means of production and the socialisation of labour reach a point where they prove incompatible with their capitalist husk. This bursts asunder. The knell of capitalist private property sounds. The expropriators are expropriated.

The capitalist method of appropriation proceeding out of the capitalist method of production, and consequently capitalist private property, is the first negation of individual private property based upon individual labour. But, with the inexorability of a law of nature, capitalist production begets its own negation. It is a negation of a negation. This second negation does not reestablish private property, but it does reestablish individual property upon the basis of the acquisitions of the capitalist era; i.e. on cooperation and the common ownership of the land and of the means of production (which labour itself produces).

The transformation of scattered private property based upon individual labour into capitalist property is, of course, a far more protracted process, a far more violent and difficult process, than the transformation of capitalist private property (already, in actual fact, based upon a social method of production) into social property. In the former case we are concerned with the expropriation of the mass of the people by a few usurpers; in the latter case we are concerned with the expropriation of a few usurpers by the mass of the people.

[In a letter written in 1881, two years before his death, Marx expressed unshaken conviction:[22]]

[23] Marx, *Sel. Corr.*, p. 387. Marx was writing to a Dutch socialist, Domela Nieuwenhuis. The editor of Marx's letters supplied the words in brackets.

The general demands of the French bourgeoisie laid down be-fore 1789 were roughly just the same, *mutatis mutandis* [with cor-responding alterations] as the first immediate demands of the pro-letariat are pretty uniformly to-day in all countries with capitalist production. But had any eighteenth-century Frenchman the faint-est idea *a priori* beforehand of the way in which the demands of the French bourgeoisie would be accomplished? The doctrinaire and necessarily fantastic anticipations of the programme of action for a revolution of the future only divert us from the struggle of the present. The dream that the end of the world was at hand in-spired the early Christians in their struggle with the Roman Em-pire and gave them confidence in victory. Scientific insight into the inevitable disintegration of the dominant order of society con-tinually proceeding before our eyes, and the ever-growing passion into which the masses are scourged by the old ghosts of government —while at the same time the positive development of the means of production advances with gigantic strides—all this is a sufficient guarantee that with the moment of the outbreak of a real prole-tarian revolution there will also be given the conditions (though these are certain not to be idyllic) of its next immediate *modus operandi* [form of action]. . . .

[And Engels described the future for which he and Marx had striven, to the extent that anyone caught in a time when men were condemned not to be men might be able to find words to describe an utterly changed time:[23]]

The seizure of the means of production by society puts an end to commodity production, and therewith to the domination of the product over the producer. Anarchy in social production is re-placed by conscious organization on a planned basis. The struggle for individual existence comes to an end. And at this point man in a certain sense separates finally from the animal world, leaves the conditions of animal existence behind him and enters conditions which are really human. The conditions of existence forming man's environment, which up to now have dominated man, at this point pass under the dominion and control of man, who now for the

[24] Marx and Engels, *Sel. Works*, I, 185-86.

first time becomes the real conscious master of nature, because and in so far as he has become master of his own socialization. The laws of his own social activity, which have hitherto confronted him as extraneous laws of nature dominating him, will then be applied by man with complete understanding, and hence will be dominated by man. Men's socialization of themselves, which has hitherto stood in opposition to them as forced upon them by nature and history, will then become the voluntary act of men themselves. The objective, extraneous forces which have hitherto dominated history, will then pass under the control of men themselves. It is only from this point on that men, with full consciousness, will make their history themselves; it is only from this point on that the social causes set in motion by men will have, predominantly and in constantly increasing measure, the effects willed by men. It is humanity's leap from the realm of necessity into the realm of freedom.

CHARLES DARWIN

Charles Darwin (1809-1882) was born close enough to the eighteenth century so that he first had to establish to his own satisfaction that change was possible. He lived far enough into the nineteenth century and shared its fundamental concerns deeply enough to spend most of his career demonstrating that change meant life itself. Darwin's grandfather Erasmus (1731-1802), a physician and philosopher, propounded a grand scheme of change in thousands of eighteenth century couplets. The grandson found that his own task was to show, not that change was possible or desirable philosophically, but that it did occur, allowing plant and animal life to continue by a process of ceaseless adaptation to a ceaselessly changing environment.

Darwin's mother, a daughter of the famous pottery manufacturer Josiah Wedgwood, died when Charles was eight years old. His father, an extremely successful physician, helped Darwin to weather a number of reverses by his support, both with money and with generally tolerant concern. In this passage from an autobiographical fragment written in 1838 Darwin describes his life as a schoolboy twenty years earlier:[1]

I recollect when I was at Mr. Case's inventing a whole fabric to show how fond I was of speaking the *truth!* My invention is still so vivid in my mind, that I could almost fancy it was true, did not memory of former shame tell me it was false. I have no particularly happy or unhappy recollections of this time or earlier periods of my life. I remember well a walk I took with a boy named Ford across some fields to a farmhouse on the Church Stretton road. I do not remember any mental pursuits excepting those of collecting stones, etc., gardening, and about this time going often with

[1] *More Letters of Charles Darwin*, ed. Francis Darwin and A. C. Seward (London: John Murray, 1903), I, 4. Reprinted by permission of John Murray, Publishers, Ltd.

my father in his carriage, telling him of my lessons, and seeing
game and other wild birds, which was a great delight to me. I was
born a naturalist.

[In 1876 Darwin wrote a much longer autobiography, and again described
himself at about the age of nine:[2]]

One little event during this year has fixed itself very firmly in
my mind, and I hope that it has done so from my conscience having been afterwards sorely troubled by it; it is curious as showing
that apparently I was interested at this early age in the variability
of plants! I told another little boy . . . that I could produce variously coloured Polyanthuses and Primroses by watering them with
certain coloured fluids, which was of course a monstrous fable, and
had never been tried by me. I may here also confess that as a little
boy I was much given to inventing deliberate falsehoods, and this
was always done for the sake of causing excitement. For instance,
I once gathered much valuable fruit from my Father's trees and
hid them in the shrubbery, and then ran in breathless haste to
spread the news that I had discovered a hoard of stolen fruit.

[In 1825 Darwin left his English home and went to study medicine in
Edinburgh. His father soon realized that the boy was not meant to be a
doctor. Darwin, however, did not recall the experience as entirely a waste:[3]]

During my second year in Edinburgh I attended Jameson's lectures on Geology and Zoology, but they were incredibly dull. The
sole effect they produced on me was the determination never as
long as I lived to read a book on Geology or in any way to study
the science. Yet I feel sure that I was prepared for a philosophical
treatment of the subject; for an old Mr Cotton in Shropshire who
knew a good deal about rocks, had pointed out to me, two or three
years previously a well-known large erratic boulder in the town of
Shrewsbury, called the bell-stone; he told me that there was no rock
of the same kind nearer than Cumberland or Scotland, and he
solemnly assured me that the world would come to an end before
anyone would be able to explain how this stone came where it now

[2] *The Autobiography of Charles Darwin*, ed. Nora Barlow (New York: Harcourt, Brace & World, Inc., 1958), p. 23. Copyright © 1958 by Nora Barlow.
Reprinted by permission of Harcourt, Brace & World, Inc. and A. D. Peters & Co.
    [3] *Autobiography*, pp. 52-53.

lay. This produced a deep impression on me and I meditated over this wonderful stone. . . .

A Voyage to New Worlds

During these years Darwin came to realize that his father would bequeath to him means sufficient to make a very comfortable life possible, and perhaps this expectation checked his interest in medicine. It is more likely, though, that the young Darwin felt with increasing strength the conviction which he expressed in 1838 with great force: he was born to do the work of a naturalist, and that work would focus all eyes upon him. His father, at any rate, was determined that his son would not idle his existence away.

In 1828 Darwin began studies at the University of Cambridge intended to fit him for the clergy. Both at Edinburgh and Cambridge he became friendly with older men intensely interested in science. Geology in particular seemed a field in which new knowledge of processes of development or evolution would soon be gained. Charles Lyell (1797-1875) published the first volume of his important *Principles of Geology* in 1830; the second appeared in 1832. The work's subtitle expressed Lyell's intention of linking past and present: "An Attempt to Explain the Former Changes of the Earth's Surface by Reference to Causes Now in Operation."

One of Darwin's teachers, John Stevens Henslow, encouraged him to apply for a place on a ship sailing round the world on a charting mission for the British government. Darwin's father reluctantly but eventually gave his permission for the trip, which began at the end of 1831 and lasted until October 1836. Darwin took Lyell's first volume with him, and received the second after it appeared. He found them extremely valuable in his work as the ship's naturalist. The enormous change which the five years away from England made in his life was clear to him as, vastly honored and esteemed, he wrote in 1876:[4]

The voyage of the *Beagle* has been by far the most important event in my life and has determined my whole career. . . . I have always felt that I owe to the voyage the first real training or

[4] *Autobiography*, pp. 76-79.

education of my mind. I was led to attend closely to several branches of natural history, and thus my powers of observation were improved, though they were already fairly developed. . . .

Looking backwards, I can now perceive how my love for science gradually preponderated over every other taste. During the first two years my old passion for shooting survived in nearly full force, and I shot myself all the birds and animals for my collection; but gradually I gave up my gun more and more, and finally altogether to my servant, as shooting interfered with my work, more especially with making out the geological structure of a country. I discovered, though unconsciously and insensibly, that the pleasure of observing and reasoning was a much higher one than that of skill and sport. The primeval instincts of the barbarian slowly yielded to the acquired tastes of the civilized man. That my mind became developed through my pursuits during the voyage, is rendered probable by a remark made by my father, who was the most acute observer whom I ever saw, of a sceptical disposition, and far from being a believer in phrenology; for on first seeing me after the voyage, he turned round to my sisters and exclaimed, "Why, the shape of his head is quite altered." . . .

[In his autobiography Darwin described in very considerable detail his gradual loss of religious faith between 1836 and 1839. His wife was shocked and asked their son to suppress some passages when he was editing the manuscript after his father's death. Only recently has the full text of the autobiography appeared. The vigor with which Darwin recounted the fascinating story of his crisis may cause that crisis to appear, as similar turning points do in the lives of other nineteenth-century men, a real cause of Darwin's subsequent findings. The protests of those with religious sensibilities outraged by *The Origin of Species* may also lead to the belief that Darwin opposed religion, and that his opposition enabled him to discover a new weapon against faith.

Darwin himself may have shared this view, but, if one considers him as an interpreter of change along with other such interpreters, it is clear that he may have misunderstood the effects of what he was doing. He simply refused to accept God as the Establisher of change because God could not help him understand the rocks and plants and animals which absorbed him. Connecting God to a particular lichen or mole was cumbersome and yielded no really interesting results. So Darwin abandoned God and let his concern with explaining change lead where it might. He may have felt that his crisis freed him from believing in the old God. Actually it marked his recognition that the problem of *how* change really took place, the problem of the nineteenth century, was his. The past was the past, and could speculate on the possibility of change; the present witnessed change as very real, and had to understand it.[5]]

During these two years I was led to think much about religion. Whilst on board the *Beagle* I was quite orthodox, and I remember being heartily laughed at by several of the officers (though themselves orthodox) for quoting the Bible as an unanswerable authority on some point of morality. I suppose it was the novelty of the argument that amused them. But I had gradually come, by this time, to see that the Old Testament from its manifestly false history of the world, with the Tower of Babel, the rainbow as a sign, etc., etc., and from its attributing to God the feelings of a revengeful tyrant, was no more to be trusted than the sacred books of the Hindoos, or the beliefs of any barbarian. The question then continually rose before my mind and would not be banished,—is it credible that if God were now to make a revelation to the Hindoos, would he permit it to be connected with the belief in Vishnu, Siva, &c., as Christianity is connected with the Old Testament. This appeared to me utterly incredible.

By further reflecting that the clearest evidence would be requisite to make any sane man believe in the miracles by which Christianity is supported,—that the more we know of the fixed laws of nature the more incredible do miracles become,—that the men at that time were ignorant and credulous to a degree almost incomprehensible by us,—that the Gospels cannot be proved to have been written simultaneously with the events,—that they differ in many important details, far too important as it seemed to me to be admitted as the usual inaccuracies of eye-witnesses;—by such reflections as these, which I give not as having the least novelty or value, but as they influenced me, I gradually came to disbelieve in Christianity as a divine revelation. The fact that many false religions have spread over large portions of the earth like wild-fire had some weight with me. Beautiful as is the morality of the New Testament, it can hardly be denied that its perfection depends in part on the interpretation which we now put on metaphors and allegories.

[5] *Autobiography*, pp. 85-87, 92-96.

But I was very unwilling to give up my belief;—I feel sure of this for I can well remember often and often inventing day-dreams of old letters between distinguished Romans and manuscripts being discovered at Pompeii or elsewhere which confirmed in the most striking manner all that was written in the Gospels. But I found it more and more difficult, with free scope given to my imagination, to invent evidence which would suffice to convince me. Thus disbelief crept over me at a very slow rate, but was at last complete. The rate was so slow that I felt no distress, and have never since doubted even for a single second that my conclusion was correct. I can indeed hardly see how anyone ought to wish Christianity to be true; for if so the plain language of the text seems to show that the men who do not believe, and this would include my Father, Brother and almost all my best friends, will be everlastingly punished.

And this is a damnable doctrine. . . .

Another source of conviction in the existence of God . . . follows from the extreme difficulty or rather impossibility of conceiving this immense and wonderful universe, including man with his capacity of looking far backwards and far into futurity, as the result of blind chance or necessity. When thus reflecting I feel compelled to look to a First Cause having an intelligent mind in some degree analogous to that of man; and I deserve to be called a Theist.

This conclusion was strong in my mind about the time, as far as I can remember, when I wrote the *Origin of Species*; and it is since that time that it has very gradually with many fluctuations become weaker. . . . The mystery of the beginning of all things is insoluble by us; and I for one must be content to remain an Agnostic. . . .

Nothing is more remarkable than the spread of scepticism or rationalism during the latter half of my life. Before I was engaged to be married, my father advised me to conceal carefully my doubts, for he said that he had known extreme misery thus caused with married persons. Things went on pretty well until the wife or husband became out of health, and then some women suffered miserably by doubting about the salvation of their husbands, thus making them likewise to suffer. My father added that he had known during his whole long life only three women who were sceptics;

and it should be remembered that he knew well a multitude of persons and possessed extraordinary power of winning confidence. When I asked him who the three women were, he had to own with respect to one of them, his sister-in-law Kitty Wedgwood, that he had no good evidence, only the vaguest hints, aided by the conviction that so clear-sighted a woman could not be a believer. At the present time, with my small acquaintance, I know (or have known) several married ladies, who believe very little more than their husbands. My father used to quote an unanswerable argument, by which an old lady, a Mrs Barlow, who suspected him of unorthodoxy, hoped to convert him:—"Doctor, I know that sugar is sweet in my mouth, and I know that my Redeemer liveth."

Sketching the Basic Ideas

Darwin was rapidly coming to reject the notion that species, or groupings of similar plants and animals, did not change. The idea of species unaffected by the passing of time and shifts in surroundings could only belong to an age when change was a debatable possibility. In 1877 Darwin recalled:[6]

When I was on board the *Beagle* I believed in the permanence of species, but, as far as I can remember, vague doubts occasionally flitted across my mind. On my return home in the autumn of 1836 I immediately began to prepare my journal for publication, and then saw how many facts indicated the common descent of species, so that in July, 1837, I opened a note-book to record any facts which might bear on the question; but I did not become convinced that species were mutable until, I think, two or three years had elapsed.

[Four notebooks kept by Darwin on change within groups of apparently related animals and plants have recently been published. The jottings, often telescoped, show Darwin trying to make order out of what he knew —the staggering multiplicity of forms of life and the competition among them. Here are excerpts from his first notebook, written between July 1837 and February 1838.

The apparently rough and unfinished nature of these entries is often

---

[6] In a letter to Otto Zacharias, *More Letters*, I, 367.

only apparent, if one pays attention to the frequency with which many elements sketched here return as fundamentals of Darwin's later work: the picture of nature in constant change; the recognition of change as the price of survival; the inquiry into the meaning of any series of changes, in terms of a possible direction in which it might point; the musings on the role of death in life; the virtual dismissal of the God of tradition as far too cumbersome a mechanism for the production of change which the naturalist studies; the prospect—so thrilling for investigators—of uncovering the factors that have produced, now are producing, and will produce change; the acceptance of man's animality, accomplished by the rejection of the idea of the soul, which meant the end of special status for man among the creatures of the earth.

Other nineteenth-century thinkers deeply convinced of the importance of change sometimes sound like Darwin. What is striking in these notes of a man not yet thirty is the aggressive sense of confidence with which he not only puts down something that has flashed into his mind, but keeps after it, rephrasing it and collecting data to support it. The small boy eager to create a stir survived in the older Darwin. Because he was not a conventionally good student he escaped excessive indoctrination into one vocation or the systems of a few teachers. With equal good fortune he had managed to be born into a family generally inclined to allow him to be what he wanted to be, an investigator of change in nature.[7]]

We *know* world subject to cycle of change, temperature and all circumstances, which influence living beings.

We see the young of living beings become permanently changed or subject to variety, according to circumstance,—seeds of plants sown in rich soil, many kinds are produced, though new individuals produced by buds are constant; hence we see generation here seems a means to vary or adaptation.—Again we know, in course of generation even mind and instinct becomes influenced. . . .

Each species changes. Does it progress.

Man gains ideas.

[7] "Darwin's notebooks on transmutation of species," ed. Sir Gavin de Beer, *Bulletin of the British Museum (Natural History). Historical Series*, II (1960), 27, 43, 49, 53, 68, 69. Reprinted by permission of the Trustees, British Museum (Natural History); Sir Gavin de Beer; G. P. Darwin. The notebooks are the property of Cambridge University Library and have been made available by the Librarian. Vertical lines indicating the end of a manuscript page have been omitted. All bracketed insertions in the text are Sir Gavin's.

The simplest cannot help becoming more complicated; and if we look to first origin, there must be progress. . . .

With this tendency to change (and to multiplication when isolated) requires death of species to keep numbers of forms equable. But is there any reason for supposing number of forms equable: This being due to subdivisions and amount of differences, so forms would be about equally numerous.—

Change not result of will of animal, but law of adaptation as much as acid and alkali.

Organized beings represent a tree, *irregularly branched;* some branches far more branched,—hence genera.—As many terminal buds dying, as new ones generated. There is nothing stranger in death of species, than individuals. . . .

It is a wonderful fact—Horse, Elephant and Mastodon dying out about same time in such different quarters.—Will Mr Lyell say that some[8] circumstance killed it [them] over a tract from Spain to S. America?—(*Never*).[9] They die, without they change, like golden Pippins; it is a *generation* of *species* like generation of *individuals.—*

Why does individual die? To perpetuate certain peculiarities (therefore adaptation), and to obliterate accidental varieties, and to accomodate itself to change (for, of course change even in varieties is accomodation). Now this argument applies to species.—If individual cannot procreate, he has no issue; so with species. . . .

Astronomers might formerly have said that God ordered each planet to move in its particular destiny. In same manner God orders each animal created with certain form in certain country, but how much more simple and sublime power let attraction act according to certain law, such are inevitable consequences—let animal be created, then by the fixed laws of generation, such will be their successors. Let the powers of transportal be such, and so will be the

---

[8] Printed "some [same?]" in "A Transcription of Darwin's First Notebook on Transmutation of Species," ed. Paul H. Barrett, *Bulletin of the Museum of Comparative Zoology at Harvard College,* 122 (1960), 258; and also in *The Life and Letters of Charles Darwin,* ed. Francis Darwin (New York: D. Appleton and Co., 1888), I, 369.

[9] Barrett, *Bull. Mus. Comp. Zool.,* 122:258, transcribes this as "*Never!*" and explains that "without," in the next sentence, means "unless."

forms of one country to another.—Let geological changes go at such a rate, so will be the number and distribution of the species!! . . . If my theory true, . . . We may foretell species, limits of good species being known. . . .

It leads to [knowledge of] nature of physical change between one group of animals and a successive one.—It leads to knowledge what kinds of structure may pass into each other; now on this view no one need look for intermediate structure, say in brain, between lowest mammal and reptile (or between extremities of any great divisions); thus a knowledge of possible changes is discovered, for speculating on future. . . .

With belief of transmutation and geographical grouping we are led to endeavour to discover *causes* of changes. . . . My theory would give zest to recent and fossil Comparative Anatomy; it would lead to study of instincts, heredity and mind heredity, whole [of] metaphysics.—It would lead to closest examination of hybridity,— to what circumstances favour crossing and what prevent it; and generation, causes of change in order to know what we have come from and to what we tend, this and direct examination of direct passages of structure in species might lead to laws of change, which would then be [the] main object of study, to guide our speculations with respect to past and future. . . .

The soul by consent of all is superadded, animals not got it, not look forward. If we choose to let conjecture run wild, then animals —our fellow brethren in pain, disease, death, suffering and famine, our slaves in the most laborious works, our companions in our amusements,—they may partake from our origin in one common ancestor, we may be all netted together.—

[In Darwin's second notebook on the nature of change in species, which he began in February 1838, he clearly rejected traditional concern with the problem of creation. Looking at the world with nineteenth-century eyes, he beheld man situated as no earlier age would have placed him. Probably no better forecast of Darwin's later achievement can be found than the excitement pulsing through the passage in which Darwin saw man as finished with heeding the divine voice in the heavens, and ready to abandon his special status. Man—civilized, rational man—would take his place in nature beside the apes and savages. Marx, too, had understood the need to treat man as part of nature, without any exceptions for a

supposed soul or an alleged divine origin. Man would then become a
problem for men to ponder, not for God to solve or declare insoluble.
Darwin's excitement, then, comes from a realization that he had seen the
real problem of his age, and from a very deep sense that he could deal
successfully with it.[10]]

. . . It is useless to speculate not only about beginning of animal life generally, but even about great division. Our question is
not how there come to be fishes & quadrupeds but how there come
to be many genera of fish &c. &c. at present day. . . .

Look abroad, study gradation, study unity of type, study geographical distribution, study relation of fossil with recent. The
fabric falls! But man—wonderful man "divino ore versum coelum
attentior" is an exception.—He is mammalian,—his origin has not
been indefinite.—he is not a deity, his end under present form will
come, (or how dreadfully we are deceived) then he is no exception.
—He possesses some of the same general instincts all & feelings as
animals. They on other hand can reason—but man has reasoning
powers in excess, instead of definite instincts—this is a replacement
in mental machinery so analogous to what we see in bodily, that it
does not stagger me.—What circumstances may have been necessary
to have made man! Seclusion want &c & perhaps a train of animals
of hundred generations of species to produce contingents proper.—
Present monkeys might not,—but probably would,—the world now
being fit, for such an animal—man, (rude uncivilized man) might
not have lived when certain other animals were alive, which have
perished. Let man visit Ourang-outang in domestication, hear expressive whine, see its intelligence when spoken [to], as if it understood every word said—see its affection to those it knows,—see its
passion & rage, sulkiness & very extreme of despair; let him look at
savage, roasting his parent, naked, artless, not improving, yet im-
provable and then let him dare to boast of his proud preemi-
nence. . . .

[The following is an excerpt from a philosophical notebook which Darwin
kept between July 15 and October 2, 1838. Certainly he did not separate
his concern as a naturalist from his preoccupations as a philosopher in-
quiring into the meaning of life. Had he made a rigid separation of that
kind, he probably would have settled contentedly for much smaller an-

[10] *Bull. Brit. Museum*, II, 88, 91.

swers to the great problem of change. By studying nature as known to the naturalist and typified in the baboon, he would gain more for philosophy than Locke, and by glimpsing an explanation of man's origin, to be expanded and finished in decades to come, he would benefit men more truly and lastingly than any religious revelation.[11]]

Origin of man now proved. Metaphysics must flourish. He who understands baboon would do more toward metaphysics than Locke.

[Darwin enjoyed being audacious. Another excerpt from his second species notebook could only have been written by someone who once had been a small boy eager to draw attention to himself, someone living as an adult in an age when pointing to a material base for religious belief still seemed daring:[12]]

Thought (or desires more properly) being hereditary it is difficult to imagine it anything but structure of brain hereditary, analogy points out to this.—Love of the deity effect of organization, oh you materialist! . . . Why is thought being a secretion of brain, more wonderful than gravity a property of matter? It is our arrogance, it our admiration of ourselves.

[Throughout most of his life Darwin generally used the same explanation of how his mind worked, an explanation which is important because it affected the organization of *The Origin of Species*. Between July and October 1838, Darwin observed, in his third notebook on change in species, that he frequently worked by induction, building a general principle from specific instances and then turning that principle on cases as yet unexplained. Darwin's view of his mental functioning slighted the effect of sudden visions of answers: these often led him to the tiresome collection of facts. Hunches came to him, and he welcomed them, because he believed that the world made sense as a product of changes which he could and would understand.[13]]

Mine is a bold theory, which attempts to explain, or asserts to be explicable every instinct in animals. . . .

What a magnificent view one can take of the world Astronomical

---

[11] Paul H. Barrett, "From Darwin's Unpublished Notebooks," *Centennial Review of Arts and Science,* III (1959), 403. Reprinted by permission of Paul H. Barrett, *Centennial Review,* G. P. Darwin, and the Librarian of Cambridge University. The notebook quoted is the property of the University.

[12] *Bull. Brit. Museum,* II, 101.

[13] *Bull. Brit. Museum,* II, 132, 142.

causes modified by unknown ones, cause changes in geography & changes of climate suspended to change of climate from physical causes,—then suspended changes of form in the organic world, as adaptation, & these changing affect each other, & their bodies by certain laws of harmony keep perfect in these themselves.—instincts alter, reason is formed & the world peopled with myriads of distinct forms from a period short of eternity to the present time, to the future. . . .

The line of argument often pursued throughout my theory is to establish a point as a probability by induction, & to apply it as hypotheses to other points, & see whether it will solve them.

[The outlines of the theory of change on which Darwin worked for the rest of his life were complete a few years after the end of the *Beagle* voyage. Organisms naturally struggled against each other; each differed slightly from its fellows, and as the struggle went on and on, some differences among individuals increased chances for survival, and others made destruction more likely. Just as the domestic breeder preferred some pigeons or roses to others and encouraged their increase, so nature chose some and rejected others.

When Darwin read Malthus, in October 1838, the economist's picture of hordes of creatures struggling for limited amounts of food struck him at once. In 1859 he wrote to Alfred Russel Wallace, the naturalist whose independent discovery of Darwin's leading idea in the 1850s finally spurred Darwin to publish:[14]]

. . . You are right, that I came to the conclusion that selection was the principle of change from the study of domesticated productions; and then, reading Malthus, I saw at once how to apply this principle. Geographical distribution and geological relations of extinct to recent inhabitants of South America first led me to the subject: especially the case of the Galapagos Islands.

[Malthus helped Darwin visualize the world as the stage for ceaseless struggle, but it is not likely that he supplied any major part of Darwin's theory. Entries in the last of these early notebooks on the formation of species, written between October 1838 and July 1839, show how fully Darwin had come to accept a nineteenth-century view of change. Separate sexes, for example, arose not from a divine act or a philosophical necessity, but in the course of long conflict, and they persisted because sexual reproduction lessened the number of actual species and increased the probability that some existing species would survive. It is also clear that Darwin saw "nature" merely as an expression: no superhuman figure cared about the outcome of the war which Darwin reported raging everywhere. In fact, man as a selective breeder of domesticated plants and animals came very close to doing what God would have done, if there had been a divine creator. For that reason, Darwin constantly used evidence from the experience of farmers, gardeners, and hobbyists such as pigeon fanciers, of whom he was one. In their work he found the clearest and most easily observable analogue to the process by which species arise in wild nature.[15]]

When discussing extinction of animals in Europe; the forms themselves have been basis of argument of change.—now take greater area of water & snow-line descent. I do not wish to say only cause, but one great final cause, nothing probably exists for one cause. My theory gives great final cause of sexes in separate animals: for otherwise there would be as many species, as individuals, & though we may not trace out all the ill effects,—we see it is not the order in this perfect world, either at the present, or many anterior epochs.—but we can see if all species, there would not be social animals. hence not social instincts, which as I hope to show is probably the foundation of all that is most beautiful in the moral sentiments of the animated beings—&c. this[16] is stated too strongly. for there would be innumerable species & hence few only social there could not be one body of animals. life with certainly another

Whether he was or not He is [at] present a social animal. If man is *one* great object for which the world was brought into present state,—a fact few will dispute, (although, that it was the sole object, I will dispute, when I hear from the geologist the history, from the astronomer that the moon probably is uninhabited) & if my theory be true then the formation of sexes rigidly necessary.—

Without sexual crossing, there would be endless changes, & hence no feature would be deeply impressed on it, & hence there could not be *improvement*, & hence not in higher animals—it was absolutely necessary that Physical changes should act not on individuals,

[15] *Bull. Brit. Museum,* II, 163, 164, 167, 168, 173.
[16] The words from here to the end of the paragraph are inserted between lines, and the last four words are uncertain. Perhaps "purpose" was intended at the end. [Note by Sir Gavin de Beer.]

but on masses of individuals.—so that the changes should be slow & bear relation to the whole changes of country, & not to the local changes—this could only be effected by sexes. . . .

When the laws of change are known—then primary forms may be speculated on, & laws of life,—the end of Natural History will be approximated to. . . .

It is a beautiful part of my theory, that domesticated races of organics are made by precisely same means as species—but latter far more perfectly & infinitely slower.—No domesticated animal is perfectly adapted to external conditions. . . .

By birth the successive modifications of structure being added to the germ, at a time (as even in childhood) when the organization is pliable, such modifications become as much fixed, as if added to old individuals during thousands of centuries,—each of us then is as old as the oldest animal,[17] have passed through as many changes as has every species. . . .

It is difficult to believe in the dreadful but quiet war of organic beings going on [in] the peaceful woods & smiling fields.—we must recollect the multitude of plants introduced into our gardens (opportunities of escape for foreign buds & insects) which are propagated with very little care,—& which might spread themselves as well as our wild plants, we see how full nature, how finely each holds its place.

The Origin of Species *and Fame*

In 1839 Darwin married his cousin Emma Wedgwood, daughter of the second Josiah Wedgwood. In 1842 they left London and settled in a country house at Down. Darwin's health had declined steadily after his return to England. He found that on some days he could not summon enough energy to work at all, and a few hours commonly marked the greatest extent of what he could manage to do. He suffered also from a variety of stomach complaints. According to one view, Darwin was a neurotic: his illness might symbolize punishment for the defiant newness of his theory; according to another, Darwin had picked up a tropical parasite, probably in South America, and

[17] The words "is as old as the oldest animal" were crossed out by Darwin in MS. . . . [Note by Sir Gavin de Beer.]

its ravages produced his often incapacitating symptoms. No really satisfactory explanation for Darwin's illness has yet been given. The undeniable fact is that he accomplished a great deal, both in gathering material and in writing up his findings. The nineteenth century knew many apparent invalids, or semi-invalids, who still managed to produce more significant work than their more robust successors in the following century.

Darwin's illness would have prevented him from holding a job, and luckily he did not have to. Both he and his wife had comfortable incomes which he invested profitably. His wife's careful arrangement of the details of his life allowed him to do a limited amount of concentrated work on most days, and his devoted friends kept him in touch with the scientific community.

By June 1842 he had written a thirty-five page sketch of his theory about species, and in 1844 he made a much more extensive attempt to set down both argument and evidence. In that year he described what he had been doing in a letter to his friend J. D. Hooker, a botanist:[18]

Besides a general interest about the southern lands, I have been now ever since my return engaged in a very presumptuous work, and I know no one individual who would not say a very foolish one. I was so struck with the distribution of the Galapagos organisms, &c. &c., and with the character of the American fossil mammifers, &c. &c., that I determined to collect blindly every sort of fact, which could bear any way on what are species. I have read heaps of agricultural and horticultural books, and have never ceased collecting facts. At last gleams of light have come, and I am almost convinced (quite contrary to the opinion I started with) that species are not (it is like confessing a murder) immutable. Heaven forfend me from Lamarck nonsense of a "tendency to progression," "adaptations from the slow willing of animals," &c.! But the conclusions I am led to are not widely different from his; though the means of change are wholly so. I think I have found out (here's presumption!) the simple way by which species become exquisitely adapted to various ends. You will now groan, and think to your-

[18] *Life and Letters,* I, 384. Reprinted by permission of John Murray, Publishers, Ltd., publisher of the original edition.

self, "on what a man have I been wasting my time and writing to."
I should, five years ago, have thought so. . . .

[In July, 1844, Darwin wrote a letter directing his wife to publish his
longer sketch if he died before he could expand it into an even larger
and more convincing book.[19]]

I have just finished my sketch of my species theory. If, as I believe, my theory in time be accepted even by one competent judge,
it will be a considerable step in science.

[Yet Darwin held back from making his theory public; he devoted most
of the following decade to studying intricacies of structure in barnacles.
In 1848 he justified his conduct in a letter to his teacher Henslow, who
had sent him a copy of a lecture to a society established for educating the
working classes in science:[20]]

. . . I rather demur to one sentence of yours—viz., "However
delightful any scientific pursuit may be, yet, if it should be wholly
unapplied, it is of no more use than building castles in the air."
Would not your hearers infer from this that the practical use of
each scientific discovery ought to be immediate and obvious to make
it worthy of admiration? What a beautiful instance chloroform is
of a discovery made from purely scientific researches, afterwards
coming almost by chance into practical use! For myself I would,
however, take higher ground, for I believe there exists, and I feel
within me, an instinct for truth, or knowledge or discovery, of something of the same nature as the instinct of virtue, and that our
having such an instinct is reason enough for scientific researches
without any practical results ever ensuing from them. You will
wonder what makes me run on so, but I have been working very
hard for the last eighteen months on the anatomy, etc., of the
Cirripedia (on which I shall publish a monograph), and some of
my friends laugh at me, and I fear the study of the Cirripedia will
ever remain "wholly unapplied," and yet I feel that such study is
better than castle-building.

[From the findings of the *Beagle* years to the propositions of the notebooks; from the accumulation of data that might illustrate those proposi-

[19] *Life and Letters*, I, 377.
[20] *More Letters*, I, 61-62.

tions—to what new statement? Darwin felt that only a gigantic book could adequately enclose his message. He sensed that many in his audience still thought that the question which really mattered was the eighteenth century's inquiry: is change or development or evolution possible? He would have to draw them to his nineteenth-century solution of a nineteenth-century problem: *how* does change take place?

The audacious boy and the supremely confident young man in his twenties seem to have given way to a colorless and easily panicked mole, endlessly collecting facts for a purpose all but forgotten. Yet perhaps Darwin had adopted the right strategy. He had outlined a theory, and he would do more than draw his audience to it. He would let a good part of the weight of his evidence press on them, and then they would have to answer: do you live in the nineteenth century, or not? [21]]

. . . The Cirripedes form a highly varying and difficult group of species to class; and my work was of considerable use to me, when I had to discuss in the *Origin of Species* the principles of a natural classification. Nevertheless, I doubt whether the work was worth the consumption of so much time.

From September 1854 onwards I devoted all my time to arranging my huge pile of notes, to observing, and experimenting, in relation to the transmutation of species. During the voyage of the *Beagle* I had been deeply impressed by discovering in the Pampean formation great fossil animals covered with armour like that on the existing armadillos; secondly, by the manner in which closely allied animals replace one another in proceeding southwards over the Continent; and thirdly, by the South American character of most of the productions of the Galapagos archipelago, and more especially by the maner in which they differ slightly on each island of the group; none of these islands appearing to be very ancient in a geological sense.

It was evident that such facts as these, as well as many others, could be explained on the supposition that species gradually become modified; and the subject haunted me. But it was equally evident that neither the action of the surrounding conditions, nor the will of the organisms (especially in the case of plants), could account for the innumerable cases in which organisms of every kind are beautifully adapted to their habits of life,—for instance, a wood-

[21] *Autobiography,* pp. 118-122.

pecker or tree-frog to climb trees, or a seed for dispersal by hooks or plumes. I had always been much struck by such adaptations, and until these could be explained it seemed to me almost useless to endeavour to prove by indirect evidence that species have been modified.

After my return to England it appeared to me that by following the example of Lyell in Geology, and by collecting all facts which bore in any way on the variation of animals and plants under domestication and nature, some light might perhaps be thrown on the whole subject. My first note-book was opened in July 1837. I worked on true Baconian principles, and without any theory collected facts on a wholesale scale, more especially with respect to domesticated productions, by printed enquiries, by conversation with skilful breeders and gardeners, and by extensive reading. When I see the list of books of all kinds which I read and abstracted, including whole series of Journals and Transactions, I am surprised at my industry. I soon perceived that selection was the keystone of man's success in making useful races of animals and plants. But how selection could be applied to organisms living in a state of nature remained for some time a mystery to me.

In October 1838, that is, fifteen months after I had begun my systematic enquiry, I happened to read for amusement Malthus on *Population,* and being well prepared to appreciate the struggle for existence which everywhere goes on from long-continued observation of the habits of animals and plants, it at once struck me that under these circumstances favourable variations would tend to be preserved, and unfavourable ones to be destroyed. The result of this would be the formation of new species. Here, then, I had at last got a theory by which to work; but I was so anxious to avoid prejudice, that I determined not for some time to write even the briefest sketch of it. In June 1842 I first allowed myself the satisfaction of writing a very brief abstract of my theory in pencil in 35 pages; and this was enlarged during the summer of 1844 into one of 230 pages, which I had fairly copied out and still possess.

But at that time I overlooked one problem of great importance; and it is astonishing to me, except on the principle of Columbus and his egg, how I could have overlooked it and its solution. This problem is the tendency in organic beings descended from the same stock to diverge in character as they become modified. That they have diverged greatly is obvious from the manner in which species of all kinds can be classed under genera, genera under families, families under sub-orders, and so forth; and I can remember the very spot in the road, whilst in my carriage, when to my joy the solution occurred to me; and this was long after I had come to Down. The solution, as I believe, is that the modified offspring of all dominant and increasing forms tend to become adapted to many and highly diversified places in the economy of nature.

Early in 1856 Lyell advised me to write out my views pretty fully, and I began at once to do so on a scale three or four times as extensive as that which was afterwards followed in my *Origin of Species;* yet it was only an abstract of the materials which I had collected, and I got through about half the work on this scale. But my plans were overthrown, for early in the summer of 1858 Mr Wallace,[22] who was then in the Malay archipelago, sent me an essay *On the Tendency of Varieties to depart indefinitely from the Original Type;* and this essay contained exactly the same theory as mine. Mr Wallace expressed the wish that if I thought well of his essay, I should send it to Lyell for perusal.

The circumstances under which I consented at the request of Lyell and Hooker to allow of an extract from my MS., together with a letter to Asa Gray, dated September 5, 1857, to be published at the same time with Wallace's Essay, are given in the *Journal of the Proceedings of the Linnean Society,* 1858, p. 45. I was at first very unwilling to consent, as I thought Mr Wallace might consider my doing so unjustifiable, for I did not then know how generous and noble was his disposition. The extract from my MS. and the letter to Asa Gray had neither been intended for publication, and were badly written. Mr Wallace's essay, on the other hand, was admirably expressed and quite clear. Nevertheless, our joint productions excited very little attention, and the only published notice of them which I can remember was by Professor Haughton of Dublin, whose verdict was that all that was new in them was false,

[22] Alfred Russel Wallace, 1823-1913, naturalist and traveller, author of various works on geographical distribution and evolution. F.R.S. 1893. [Note by editor of Darwin's *Autobiography*.]

and what was true was old. This shows how necessary it is that any new view should be explained at considerable length in order to arouse public attention.

[In spite of Darwin's disclaimer, the extract from his manuscript stated his case admirably. Actually, it was part of the long essay which he drafted in 1844. The heading of his 1858 publication indicated the most important parts of his argument: "On the Variation of Organic Beings in a State of Nature; On the Natural Means of Selection; On the Comparison of Domestic Races and True Species:" [23]]

De Candolle, in an eloquent passage, has declared that all nature is at war, one organism with another, or with external nature. Seeing the contented face of nature, this may at first well be doubted: but reflection will inevitably prove it to be true. The war, however, is not constant, but recurrent in a slight degree at short periods, and more severely at occasional more distant periods; and hence its effects are easily overlooked. It is the doctrine of Malthus applied in most cases with tenfold force. As in every climate there are seasons, for each of its inhabitants, of greater and less abundance, so all annually breed; and the moral restraint which in some small degree checks the increase of mankind is entirely lost. Even slow-breeding mankind has doubled in twenty-five years; and if he could increase his food with greater ease, he would double in less time. But for animals without artificial means, the amount of food for each species must, *on an average,* be constant, whereas the increase of all organisms tends to be geometrical, and in a vast majority of cases at an enormous ratio. Suppose in a certain spot there are eight pairs of birds, and that *only* four pairs of them annually (including double hatches) rear only four young, and that these go on rearing their young at the same rate, then at the end of seven years (a short life, excluding violent deaths, for any bird) there will be 2048 birds, instead of the original sixteen. As this increase is quite impossible, we must conclude either that birds do not rear nearly half their young, or that the average life of a bird is, from accident, not nearly

[23] Charles Darwin and Alfred Russel Wallace, *Evolution by Natural Selection,* ed. Sir Gavin de Beer (Cambridge: At the University Press, 1958), pp. 259-63. Reprinted by permission of The Linnean Society, London, and the Johnson Reprint Corporation, Limited.

seven years. Both checks probably concur. The same kind of calculation applied to all plants and animals affords results more or less
striking, but in very few instances more striking than in man.

Many practical illustrations of this rapid tendency to increase are
on record, among which, during peculiar seasons, are the extraordinary numbers of certain animals; for instance, during the years
1826 to 1828, in La Plata, when from drought some millions of
cattle perished, the whole country actually *swarmed* with mice. Now
I think it cannot be doubted that during the breeding season all
the mice (with the exception of a few males or females in excess)
ordinarily pair, and therefore that this astounding increase during
three years must be attributed to a greater number than usual surviving the first year, and then breeding, and so on till the third
year, when their numbers were brought down to their usual limits
on the return of wet weather. Where man has introduced plants
and animals into a new and favourable country, there are many
accounts in how surprisingly few years the whole country has become stocked with them. This increase would necessarily stop as
soon as the country was fully stocked; and yet we have every reason
to believe, from what is known of wild animals, that *all* would pair
in the spring. In the majority of cases it is most difficult to imagine
where the check falls—though generally, no doubt, on the seeds,
eggs, and young; but when we remember how impossible, even in
mankind (so much better known than any other animal), it is to
infer from repeated casual observations what the average duration
of life is, or to discover the different percentage of deaths to births
in different countries, we ought to feel no surprise at our being
unable to discover where the check falls in any animal or plant. It
should always be remembered, that in most cases the checks are
recurrent yearly in a small, regular degree, and in an extreme degree during unusually cold, hot, dry, or wet years, according to the
constitution of the being in question. Lighten any check in the
least degree, and the geometrical powers of increase in every organism will almost instantly increase the average number of the
favoured species. Nature may be compared to a surface on which
rest ten thousand sharp wedges touching each other and driven in-
wards by incessant blows. Fully to realize these views much reflection
is requisite. Malthus on man should be studied; and all such cases

as those of the mice in La Plata, of the cattle and horses when first turned out in South America, of the birds by our calculation, etc., should be well considered. Reflect on the enormous multiplying power *inherent and annually in action* in all animals; reflect on the countless seeds scattered by a hundred ingenious contrivances, year after year, over the whole face of the land; and yet we have every reason to suppose that the average percentage of each of the inhabitants of a country usually remains constant. Finally, let it be borne in mind that this average number of individuals (the external conditions remaining the same) in each country is kept up by recurrent struggles against other species or against external nature (as on the borders of the arctic regions, where the cold checks life), and that ordinarily each individual of every species holds its place, either by its own struggle and capacity of acquiring nourishment in some period of its life, from the egg upwards; or by the struggle of its parents (in short-lived organisms, when the main check occurs at longer intervals) with other individuals of the *same* or *different* species.

But let the external conditions of a country alter. If in a small degree, the relative proportions of the inhabitants will in most cases simply be slightly changed; but let the number of inhabitants be small, as on an island, and free access to it from other countries be circumscribed, and let the change of conditions continue progressing (forming new stations), in such a case the original inhabitants must cease to be as perfectly adapted to the changed conditions as they were originally. It has been shown in a former part of this work, that such changes of external conditions would, from their acting on the reproductive system, probably cause the organization of those beings which were most affected to become, as under domestication, plastic. Now, can it be doubted, from the struggle each individual has to obtain subsistence, that any minute variation in structure, habits, or instincts, adapting that individual better to the new conditions, would tell upon its vigour and health? In the struggle it would have a better *chance* of surviving; and those of its offspring which inherited the variation, be it ever so slight, would also have a better *chance*. Yearly more are bred than can survive; the smallest grain in the balance, in the long run, must tell on which death shall fall, and which shall survive. Let this work of selection on

the one hand, and death on the other, go on for a thousand generations, who will pretend to affirm that it would produce no effect,
when we remember what, in a few years, Bakewell effected in cattle,
and Western in sheep, by this identical principle of selection?

To give an imaginary example from changes in progress on an
island: let the organization of a canine animal which preyed chiefly
on rabbits, but sometimes on hares, become slightly plastic; let these
same changes cause the number of rabbits very slowly to decrease,
and the number of hares to increase; the effect of this would be that
the fox or dog would be driven to try to catch more hares: his organization, however, being slightly plastic, those individuals with
the lightest forms, longest limbs, and best eyesight, let the difference
be ever so small, would be slightly favoured, and would tend to live
longer, and to survive during that time of the year when food was
scarcest; they would also rear more young, which would tend to
inherit these slight peculiarities. The less fleet ones would be rigidly
destroyed. I can see no more reason to doubt that these causes in
a thousand generations would produce a marked effect, and adapt
the form of the fox or dog to the catching of hares instead of rabbits,
than that greyhounds can be improved by selection and carefui
breeding. So would it be with plants under similar circumstances.
If the number of individuals of a species with plumed seeds could
be increased by greater powers of dissemination within its own area
(that is, if the check to increase fell chiefly on the seeds), those seeds
which were provided with ever so little more down, would in the
long run be most disseminated; hence a greater number of seeds
thus formed would germinate, and would tend to produce plants
inheriting the slightly better-adapted down.[24]

Besides this natural means of selection, by which those individuals are preserved, whether in their egg, or larval, or mature state,
which are best adapted to the place they fill in nature, there is a
second agency at work in most unisexual animals, tending to produce the same effect, namely the struggle of the males for the females. These struggles are generally decided by the law of battle,
but in the case of birds, apparently, by the charms of their song,
by their beauty or their power of courtship, as in the dancing rock-

[24] I can see no more difficulty in this, than in the planter improving his
varieties of the cotton plant. [Note by Darwin, 1858.]

thrush of Guiana. The most vigorous and healthy males, implying perfect adaptation, must generally gain the victory in their contests. This kind of selection, however, is less rigorous than the other; it does not require the death of the less successful, but gives to them fewer descendants. The struggle falls, moreover, at a time of year when food is generally abundant, and perhaps the effect chiefly produced would be the modification of the secondary sexual characters, which are not related to the power of obtaining food, or to defence from enemies, but to fighting with or rivalling other males. The result of this struggle amongst the males may be compared in some respects to that produced by those agriculturists, who pay less attention to the careful selection of all their young animals, and more to the occasional use of a choice male.

[Faced with the prospect of being deprived of the center of the stage, Darwin underwent a kind of inner rallying. The support of his friends helped him to overcome ill health. Perhaps they represented part of the audience which he had so long imagined was waiting to listen to him. Certainly he worked as vigorously as any man in good health, and as effectively. In his *Autobiography* he wrote, at the end of the long passage just quoted:]

In September 1858 I set to work by the strong advice of Lyell and Hooker to prepare a volume on the transmutation of species, but was often interrupted by ill-health, and short visits to Dr. Lane's delightful hydropathic establishment at Moor Park. I abstracted the MS. begun on a much larger scale in 1856, and completed the volume on the same reduced scale. It cost me thirteen months and ten days' hard labour. It was published under the title of the *Origin of Species*, in November 1859. Though considerably added to and corrected in the later editions, it has remained substantially the same book.

[In the final chapter of *The Origin* Darwin indicated the distance he had traveled and emphasized the new vistas his work opened, as he had hoped in his notebooks on species, written in the 1830s:[25]]

[25] *The Origin of Species By Means of Natural Selection or the Preservation of Favoured Races in the Struggle for Life* (New York: Washington Square Press, Inc., 1958), pp. 461, 464-70. Reprinted by permission of John Murray, Publishers, Ltd.

I have now recapitulated the facts and considerations which have thoroughly convinced me that species have been modified, during a long course of descent. This has been effected chiefly through the natural selection of numerous successive, slight, favourable variations; aided in an important manner by the inherited effects of the use and disuse of parts; and in an unimportant manner, that is in relation to adaptive structures, whether past or present, by the direct action of external conditions, and by variations which seem to us in our ignorance to arise spontaneously. . . .

It may be asked how far I extend the doctrine of the modification of species. . . .

Organs in a rudimentary condition plainly show that an early progenitor had the organ in a fully developed condition; and this in some cases implies an enormous amount of modification in the descendants. Throughout whole classes various structures are formed on the same pattern, and at a very early age the embryos closely resemble each other. Therefore I cannot doubt that the theory of descent with modification embraces all the members of the same great class or kingdom. I believe that animals are descended from at most only four or five progenitors, and plants from an equal or lesser number.

When the views advanced by me in this volume, and by Mr. Wallace, or when analogous views on the origin of species are generally admitted, we can dimly foresee that there will be a considerable revolution in natural history. . . .

When we no longer look at an organic being as a savage looks at a ship, as something wholly beyond his comprehension; when we regard every production of nature as one which has had a long history; when we contemplate every complex structure and instinct as the summing up of many contrivances, each useful to the possessor, in the same way as any great mechanical invention is the summing up of the labour, the experience, the reason, and even the blunders of numerous workmen; when we thus view each organic being, how far more interesting—I speak from experience—does the study of natural history become! . . .

In the future I see open fields for far more important researches. Psychology will be securely based on the foundation already well laid by Mr. Herbert Spencer, that of the necessary acquirement of each mental power and capacity by gradation. Much light will be thrown on the origin of man and his history.

Authors of the highest eminence seem to be fully satisfied with the view that each species has been independently created. To my mind it accords better with what we know of the laws impressed on matter by the Creator, that the production and extinction of the past and present inhabitants of the world should have been due to secondary causes, like those determining the birth and death of the individual. When I view all beings not as special creations, but as the lineal descendants of some few beings which lived long before the first bed of the Cambrian system was deposited, they seem to me to become ennobled. Judging from the past, we may safely infer that not one living species will transmit its unaltered likeness to a distant futurity. And of the species now living very few will transmit progeny of any kind to a far distant futurity; for the manner in which all organic beings are grouped, shows that the greater number of species in each genus, and all the species in many genera, have left no descendants, but have become utterly extinct. We can so far take a prophetic glance into futurity as to foretell that it will be the common and widely-spread species, belonging to the larger and dominant groups within each class, which will ultimately prevail and procreate new and dominant species. As all the living forms of life are the lineal descendants of those which lived long before the Cambrian epoch, we may feel certain that the ordinary succession by generation has never once been broken, and that no cataclysm has desolated the whole world. Hence we may look with some confidence to a secure future of great length. And as natural selection works solely by and for the good of each being, all corporeal and mental endowments will tend to progress towards perfection.

It is interesting to contemplate a tangled bank, clothed with many plants of many kinds, with birds singing on the bushes, with various insects flitting about, and with worms crawling through the damp earth, and to reflect that these elaborately constructed forms, so different from each other, and dependent upon each other in so complex a manner, have all been produced by laws acting around us. These laws, taken in the largest sense, being Growth with Reproduction; Inheritance which is almost implied by reproduction;

Variability from the indirect and direct action of the conditions of life, and from use and disuse: a Ratio of Increase so high as to lead to a Struggle for Life, and as a consequence to Natural Selection, entailing Divergence of Character and the Extinction of less-improved forms. Thus, from the war of nature, from famine and death, the most exalted object which we are capable of conceiving, namely, the production of the higher animals, directly follows. There is grandeur in this view of life, with its several powers, having been originally breathed by the Creator into a few forms or into one; and that, whilst this planet has gone cycling on according to the fixed law of gravity, from so simple a beginning endless forms most beautiful and most wonderful have been, and are being evolved.

[Darwin had a keen interest in the reasons for the success of his book, and in his autobiography he discussed them.[26]]

It is no doubt the chief work of my life. It was from the first highly successful. The first small edition of 1250 copies was sold on the day of publication, and a second edition of 3000 copies soon afterwards. Sixteen thousand copies have now (1876) been sold in England and considering how stiff a book it is, this is a large sale. It has been translated into almost every European tongue, even into such languages as Spanish, Bohemian, Polish, and Russian. It has also, according to Miss Bird, been translated into Japanese, and is there much studied.[27] Even an essay in Hebrew has appeared on it, showing that the theory is contained in the Old Testament! The reviews were very numerous; for a time I collected all that appeared on the *Origin* and on my related books, and these amount (excluding newspaper reviews) to 265; but after a time I gave up the attempt in despair. Many separate essays and books on the subject have appeared; and in Germany a catalogue or bibliography on "Darwinismus" has appeared every year or two.

The success of the *Origin* may, I think, be attributed in large part to my having long before written two condensed sketches, and to my having finally abstracted a much larger manuscript, which was itself an abstract. By this means I was enabled to select the

[26] *Autobiography*, pp. 122-24, 139-41, 144-45.
[27] Darwin's son Francis noted here that Miss Bird was mistaken.

more striking facts and conclusions. I had, also, during many years, followed a golden rule, namely, that whenever a published fact, a new observation or thought came across me, which was opposed to my general results, to make a memorandum of it without fail and at once; for I had found by experience that such facts and thoughts were far more apt to escape from the memory than favourable ones. Owing to this habit, very few objections were raised against my views which I had not at least noticed and attempted to answer.

It has sometimes been said that the success of the *Origin* proved "that the subject was in the air," or "that men's minds were prepared for it." I do not think that this is strictly true, for I occasionally sounded not a few naturalists, and never happened to come across a single one who seemed to doubt about the permanence of species. Even Lyell and Hooker, though they would listen with interest to me, never seemed to agree. I tried once or twice to explain to able men what I meant by natural selection, but signally failed. What I believe was strictly true is that innumerable well-observed facts were stored in the minds of naturalists, ready to take their proper places as soon as any theory which would receive them was sufficiently explained. . . .

My books have sold largely in England, have been translated into many languages, and passed through several editions in foreign countries. I have heard it said that the success of a work abroad is the best test of its enduring value. I doubt whether this is at all trustworthy; but judged by this standard my name ought to last for a few years. Therefore it may be worth while for me to try to analyse the mental qualities and the conditions on which my success has depended; though I am aware that no man can do this correctly.

I have no great quickness of apprehension or wit which is so remarkable in some clever men, for instance Huxley. I am therefore a poor critic: a paper or book, when first read, generally excites my admiration, and it is only after considerable reflection that I perceive the weak points. My power to follow a long and purely abstract train of thought is very limited; I should, moreover, never have succeeded with metaphysics or mathematics. My memory is extensive, yet hazy: it suffices to make me cautious by vaguely telling me that I have observed or read something opposed to the conclusion which I am drawing, or on the other hand in favour of it; and after a time I can generally recollect where to search for my authority. So poor in one sense is my memory, that I have never been able to remember for more than a few days a single date or a line of poetry.

Some of my critics have said, "Oh, he is a good observer, but has no power of reasoning." I do not think that this can be true, for the *Origin of Species* is one long argument from the beginning to the end, and it has convinced not a few able men. No one could have written it without having some power of reasoning. I have a fair share of invention and of common sense or judgment, such as every fairly successful lawyer or doctor must have, but not I believe, in any higher degree.

On the favourable side of the balance, I think that I am superior to the common run of men in noticing things which easily escape attention, and in observing them carefully. My industry has been nearly as great as it could have been in the observation and collection of facts. What is far more important, my love of natural science has been steady and ardent. This pure love has, however, been much aided by the ambition to be esteemed by my fellow naturalists. From my early youth I have had the strongest desire to understand or explain whatever I observed,—that is, to group all facts under some general laws. These causes combined have given me the patience to reflect or ponder for any number of years over any unexplained problem. As far as I can judge, I am not apt to follow blindly the lead of other men. I have steadily endeavoured to keep my mind free, so as to give up any hypothesis, however much beloved (and I cannot resist forming one on every subject), as soon as facts are shown to be opposed to it. Indeed I have had no choice but to act in this manner, for with the exception of the Coral Reefs, I cannot remember a single first-formed hypothesis which had not after a time to be given up or greatly modified. . . .

My habits are methodical, and this has been of not a little use for my particular line of work. Lastly, I have had ample leisure from not having to earn my own bread. Even ill-health, though it has annihilated several years of my life, has saved me from the distractions of society and amusement.

Therefore, my success as a man of science, whatever this may have amounted to, has been determined, as far as I can judge, by complex and diversified mental qualities and conditions. Of these the most important have been—the love of science—unbounded patience in long reflecting over any subject—industry in observing and collecting facts—and a fair share of invention as well as of common-sense. With such moderate abilities as I possess, it is truly surprising that thus I should have influenced to a considerable extent the beliefs of scientific men on some important points.

[In April, 1859, Darwin had believed that his views would win the future, but he also experienced doubts, apparent in the following letter to Wallace. Darwin could not yet count on being preferred over other theorists by Huxley, who later became his staunchest advocate.[28]]

I forget whether I told you that Hooker, who is our best British botanist, and perhaps the best in the world, is a full convert, and is now immediately going to publish his confession of faith. . . . Huxley is changed, and believes in mutation of species: whether a convert to us, I do not quite know. We shall live to see all the younger men converts.

[In a letter to Hooker, written in May 1859, Darwin made very clear that he was still the small boy determined to impress an audience through discoveries about nature, but he was that small boy grown up into a man afraid of being ridiculed if the wish hidden behind his performance were discovered:[29]]

Please do not say to anyone that I thought my book on species would be fairly popular and have a fairly remunerative sale (which was the height of my ambition), for if it prove a dead failure it would make me the more ridiculous.

[By December 1 of that year he was writing about the eagerness with which booksellers were buying from his publisher:[30]]

. . . I have lately heard from Murray that he sold at his sale far more copies than he has of the *Origin of Species,* and that I must immediately prepare a new edition, which I am now correcting. By

---

[28] *More Letters,* I, 119.
[29] *More Letters,* I, 120-21.
[30] *More Letters,* I, 123. To W. H. Miller.

the way, I hear from Murray that all the attacks heaped on my book do not seem to have at all injured the sale. . . .

[Two years later he wrote to the well-known scientist Sir John Herschel:[31]]

You will think me very conceited when I say I feel quite easy about the ultimate success of my views, (with much error, as yet unseen by me, to be no doubt eliminated); & I feel this confidence because I find so many young & middle-aged truly good workers in different branches, either partially or wholly accepting my views, because they find they can thus group & understand many scattered facts.

The Meaning of Man's Evolution

Darwin had been intensely interested in the fate of man at least as early as the notebooks on species change of the late 1830s. In the 1860s, enjoying the considerable approval which his book on species had won, he felt encouraged to examine in much greater detail the meaning of the changes which had combined to produce man. Secure in the knowledge that some scientists approved of his work, secure in the confidence that more would do so, he would not allow himself to be seriously dispirited by those who attacked him. Like a good nineteenth-century man, Darwin wanted to believe that mankind would improve:[32]

I cannot explain why, but to me it would be an infinite satisfaction to believe that mankind will progress to such a pitch that we should [look] back at [ourselves] as mere Barbarians.

[He read widely, searching for evidence which would lead him beyond hope to conviction. In 1873 he wrote to Francis Galton about W. R. Greg's *The Enigmas of Life*:[33]]

. . . I have almost finished Greg's *Enigmas*. It is grand poetry—but too Utopian and too full of faith for me; so that I have been

---

[31] Sir Gavin de Beer, "Some unpublished letters of Charles Darwin," *Notes and Records of the Royal Society of London*, XIV (1959), 35. Reprinted by permission of the Royal Society, owners of the copyright; and of Sir Gavin de Beer.

[32] *More Letters*, II, 30. To Lyell, 1860.

[33] *More Letters*, II, 44.

rather disappointed. What do you think about it? He must be a delightful man.

[Darwin had known Herbert Spencer's work for many years when he came to write *The Descent of Man*. In 1858 he had written to thank Spencer for the gift of a book:[34]]

DEAR SIR,—I beg permission to thank you sincerely for your very kind present of your Essays. I have already read several of them with much interest. Your remarks on the general argument of the so-called development theory seems to me admirable. I am at present preparing an Abstract of a larger work on the change of species; but I treat the subject simply as a naturalist, and not from a general point of view, otherwise, in my opinion, your argument could not have been improved on, and might have been quoted by me with great advantage.

[Both Darwin and Spencer refused to restrain themselves within the confines of a single subject as subjects now are understood. For that reason, no single label accurately describes their activities: they were biologists and philosophers and psychologists and anthropologists, but they did not see themselves in these ways. They sought to realize aims which transcended such professional categories, though their attainment of such large aims might vary considerably, as Darwin observed to Hooker in 1866, after reading the last installment of Spencer's *Principles of Biology*:[35]]

. . . I have now read the last No. of H. Spencer. I do not know whether to think it better than the previous number, but it is wonderfully clever, and I dare say mostly true. I feel rather mean when I read him: I could bear, and rather enjoy feeling that he was twice as ingenious and clever as myself, but when I feel that he is about a dozen times my superior, even in the master art of wriggling, I feel aggrieved. If he had trained himself to observe more, even if at the expense, by the law of balancement, of some loss of thinking power, he would have been a wonderful man.

[But in 1870 Darwin wrote to the scientist E. Ray Lankester:[36]]

[34] *Life and Letters*, I, 497.
[35] *Life and Letters*, II, 239.
[36] *Life and Letters*, II, 301.

. . . It has also pleased me to see how thoroughly you appreciate (and I do not think that this is general with the men of science) H. Spencer; I suspect that hereafter he will be looked at as by far the greatest living philosopher in England; perhaps equal to any that have lived. . . .

[By this time he had nearly finished his book on man. In his autobiography he described its composition:[37]]

My *Descent of Man* was published in Feb. 1871. As soon as I had become, in the year 1837 or 1838, convinced that species were mutable productions, I could not avoid the belief that man must come under the same law. Accordingly I collected notes on the subject for my own satisfaction, and not for a long time with any intention of publishing. Although in the *Origin of Species,* the derivation of any particular species is never discussed, yet I thought it best, in order that no honourable man should accuse me of concealing my views, to add that by the work in question "light would be thrown on the origin of man and his history." It would have been useless and injurious to the success of the book to have paraded without giving any evidence my conviction with respect to his origin.

But when I found that many naturalists fully accepted the doctrine of the evolution of species, it seemed to me advisable to work up such notes as I possessed and to publish a special treatise on the origin of man. . . .

[Few nineteenth-century books end more forcefully than *The Descent of Man.* Man had to acknowledge his animality, to admit that he was only a link in a series running from monkeys and baboons on through savages. Darwin was quite prepared for such acknowledgment, and had been prepared since his years on the *Beagle.* Darwin's life held together with marvelous consistency, so that it is strikingly appropriate for him to mention the wild Fuegians at the close of *The Descent of Man.* He had succeeded in making the greatest use possible for him of the materials which he assembled and the impressions they left in his memory. More would be done, by younger men like Freud, who would be drawn to analyze

---

[37] *Autobiography,* 130-31.

further the bonds among higher apes, savages, and civilized men formu-
lated by Darwin.[38]]

The main conclusion arrived at in this work, namely, that man is
descended from some lowly organized form, will, I regret to think,
be highly distasteful to many. But there can hardly be a doubt that
we are descended from barbarians. The astonishment which I
felt on first seeing a party of Fuegians on a wild and broken shore
will never be forgotten by me, for the reflection at once rushed into
my mind—such were our ancestors. These men were absolutely
naked and bedaubed with paint, their long hair was tangled, their
mouths frothed with excitement, and their expression was wild,
startled, and distrustful. They possessed hardly any arts, and, like
wild animals, lived on what they could catch; they had no government, and were merciless to every one not of their own small tribe.
He who has seen a savage in his native land will not feel much shame
if forced to acknowledge that the blood of some more humble creature flows in his veins. For my own part, I would as soon be
descended from that heroic little monkey who braved his dreaded
enemy in order to save the life of his keeper, or from that old baboon,
who, descending from the mountains, carried away in triumph his
young comrade from a crowd of astonished dogs—as from a savage
who delights to torture his enemies, offers up bloody sacrifices,
practices infanticide without remorse, treats his wives like slaves,
knows no decency, and is haunted by the grossest superstitions.

Man may be excused for feeling some pride at having risen,
though not through his own exertions, to the very summit of the
organic scale; and the fact of his having thus risen, instead of having
been aboriginally placed there, may give him hope for a still higher
destiny in the distant future. But we are not here concerned with
hopes or fears, only with the truth as far as our reason permits us to
discover it; and I have given the evidence to the best of my ability.
We must, however, acknowledge, as it seems to me, that man, with
all his noble qualities, with sympathy which feels for the most
debased, with benevolence which extends not only to other men but
to the humblest living creature, with his godlike intellect which has

[38] *The Descent of Man and Selection in Relation to Sex* (New York: P. F. Col-
lier and Son, 1901), II, 796-97. This is a reprinting of the second edition (1874).
Reprinted by permission of John Murray, Publishers, Ltd.

penetrated into the movements and constitution of the solar system —with all these exalted powers—Man still bears in his bodily frame the indelible stamp of his lowly origin.

[Civilized men were no less animals than were their ancestors, and so they too had to struggle.[39]]

Natural Selection as Affecting Civilized Nations.—I have hitherto only considered the advancement of man from a semi-human condition to that of the modern savage. But some remarks on the action of natural selection on civilized nations may be worth adding. This subject has been ably discussed by Mr. W. R. Greg, and previously by Mr. Wallace and Mr. Galton. Most of my remarks are taken from these three authors. With savages, the weak in body or mind are soon eliminated; and those that survive commonly exhibit a vigorous state of health. We civilized men, on the other hand, do our utmost to check the process of elimination; we build asylums for the imbecile, the maimed, and the sick; we institute poor-laws; and our medical men exert their utmost skill to save the life of every one to the last moment. There is reason to believe that vaccination has preserved thousands who from a weak constitution would formerly have succumbed to small-pox. Thus the weak members of civilized societies propagate their kind. No one who has attended to the breeding of domestic animals will doubt that this must be highly injurious to the race of man. It is surprising how soon a want of care, or care wrongly directed, leads to the degeneration of a domestic race; but, excepting in the case of man himself, hardly any one is so ignorant as to allow his worst animals to breed.

The aid which we feel impelled to give to the helpless is mainly an incidental result of the instinct of sympathy, which was originally acquired as part of the social instincts, but subsequently rendered, in the manner previously indicated, more tender and more widely diffused. Nor could we check our sympathy, even at the urging of hard reason, without deterioration in the noblest part of our nature. The surgeon may harden himself while performing an operation, for he knows that he is acting for the good of his patient; but if we were intentionally to neglect the weak and helpless, it could only be for a contingent benefit, with an overwhelming present evil. We must

---

[39] *Descent of Man,* I, 180-81.

therefore bear the undoubtedly bad effects of the weak surviving and propagating their kind; but there appears to be at least one check in steady action, namely, that the weaker and inferior members of society do not marry so freely as the sound; and this check might be indefinitely increased by the weak in body or mind refraining from marriage, though this is more to be hoped for than expected. . . .

[Affairs generally turned out for the best if men were allowed to battle among themselves as they naturally would. Some justly became wealthy, some justly remained poor:[40]]

Man accumulates property and bequeaths it to his children, so that the children of the rich have an advantage over the poor in the race for success, independently of bodily or mental superiority. On the other hand, the children of parents who are short-lived, and are therefore on an average deficient in health and vigor, come into their property sooner than other children, and will be likely to marry earlier, and leave a larger number of offspring to inherit their inferior constitutions. But the inheritance of property by itself is very far from an evil; for without the accumulation of capital the arts could not progress; and it is chiefly through their power that the civilized races have extended, and are now everywhere extending their range, so as to take the place of the lower races. Nor does the moderate accumulation of wealth interfere with the process of selection. When a poor man becomes moderately rich, his children enter trades or professions in which there is struggle enough, so that the able in body and mind succeed best. The presence of a body of well-instructed men, who have not to labor for their daily bread, is important to a degree which cannot be over-estimated; as all high intellectual work is carried on by them, and on such work material progress of all kinds mainly depends, not to mention other and higher advantages. No doubt wealth when very great tends to convert men into useless drones, but their number is never large; and some degree of elimination here occurs, for we daily see rich men, who happen to be fools or profligate, squandering away their wealth. . . .

[Like Spencer, and very much like many writers on politics sometimes supposed to be drawing wild inferences from Darwin's biological work, Dar-

[40] *Descent of Man,* I, 182.

win himself considered reflection on topics such as the probable fate of nations to be very much a proper concern. The later "social Darwinists" might point for justification of the form and content of their work to Darwin's own example:[41]]

. . . There is apparently much truth in the belief that the wonderful progress of the United States, as well as the character of the people, are the results of natural selection; for the more energetic, restless, and courageous men from all parts of Europe have emigrated during the last ten or twelve generations to that great country, and have there succeeded best. Looking to the distant future, I do not think that the Rev. Mr. Zincke takes an exaggerated view when he says: "All other series of events—as that which resulted in the culture of mind in Greece, and that which resulted in the empire of Rome—only appear to have purpose and value when viewed in connection with, or rather as subsidiary to . . . the great stream of Anglo-Saxon emigration to the west." Obscure as is the problem of the advance of civilization, we can at least see that a nation which produced during a lengthened period the greatest number of highly intellectual, energetic, brave, patriotic, and benevolent men, would generally prevail over less favored nations. . . .

[Darwin's pronouncements on politics very much displeased Marx, who admired him as the discoverer of a universal pattern of struggle in nature. Marx even appears to have tried to show that the means of production evolved as species evolved: thus the social and political struggles which Darwin accepted as inevitable would prove to be passing phenomena, inevitable only under capitalism.

In 1873 Marx sent Darwin a copy of the second German edition of the first volume of *Das Kapital*. Darwin responded:[42]]

Dear Sir

I thank you for the honour which you have done me by sending me your great work on Capital; & I heartily wish that I was more worthy to receive it, by understanding more of the deep & important subject of political economy. Though our studies have been so different, I believe that we both earnestly desire the extension of

[41] *Descent of Man*, I, 191.
[42] Transcript of a photocopy of the original, generously provided by the Marx-Engels-Lenin Institute, Moscow. Printed by permission of the Institute and of the Internationaal Instituut voor Sociale Geschiedenis, Amsterdam.

knowledge, & that this in the long run is sure to add to the happiness of mankind.

I remain Dear Sir

Yours faithfully

Charles Darwin

[In 1880 Marx offered to dedicate the unfinished second volume of *Das Kapital* to Darwin. According to nineteenth-century custom, no dedication could be made without the consent of the person whom it was meant to honor. A dedication, then, meant approval for the dedicator's work by the individual named in it.

Exactly what Marx sent Darwin as a statement of his views is not clear. Certainly Marx was not attempting to involve Darwin in an anti-religious campaign. Marx knew, from the last chapter of *The Origin of Species*, that Darwin did not want to use his scientific work to attack religion, and Marx himself was uninterested both in religion and in attacks on it.

Darwin's reply contains his reaction as a properly bourgeois Englishman to association with what he automatically considered to be militantly atheistic socialism, and his serene confidence in the scientific explanation of change which dominated his entire life:[43]]

Dear Sir

I am much obliged for your kind letter and the enclosure.—The publication in any form of your remarks on my writings really requires no consent on my part, and it would be ridiculous in me to give consent to what requires none.—I sh[ould] prefer the Part or Volume not to be dedicated to me (though I thank you for the intended honour) as this implies to a certain extent my approval of the general publication, about which I know nothing.—Moreover though I am a strong advocate for free thought on all subjects, yet it appears to me (whether rightly or wrongly) that direct arguments against christianity and theism produce hardly any effect on the

[43] The text of the letter is that given by Erhard Lucas, "Marx' und Engels' Auseinandersetzung mit Darwin. Zur Differenz zwischen Marx und Engels," *International Review of Social History*, IX (1964), 433-69; this text has been compared with a photocopy of the original provided by the Marx-Engels-Lenin Institute, Moscow. Lucas has published accurate texts of the two letters from Darwin to Marx and careful analyses of their background and meaning for the first time. The second letter is also reprinted by permission of the Marx-Engels-Lenin Institute, Moscow, and the Internationaal Instituut voor Sociale Geschiedenis, Amsterdam. At the top of the letter's first page Darwin wrote and underlined: "Private."

public; and freedom of thought is best promoted by the gradual [44] illumination of men's minds, which follows from the advance of science. It has, therefore, been always my object to avoid writing on religion, and I have confined myself to science. I may, however, have been unduly biassed by the pain which it would give some members of my family, if I aided in any way direct attacks on religion.—
I am sorry to refuse you any request, but I am old and have very little strength, and looking over proof-sheets (as I know by present experience) fatigues me much.—

I remain Dear Sir
yours faithfully
Ch. Darwin

[44] A supralinear addition.

HERBERT SPENCER

Outwardly the life of Herbert Spencer (1820-1903) lacks drama: an early struggle to become a writer, followed by success savored as a fussily cantankerous semi-invalid fiercely guarding his ideational priorities. Yet he waged one of the nineteenth century's longest battles to conquer all of the mysteries of change; his campaigns, usually fought singlehanded, resulted in a series of books considered extremely valuable in his own time. He realized before he died that he had fought largely in vain. He attacked on too vast a front with too inadequate equipment. The twentieth century, the age of Spengler and Toynbee, may sympathize with a man who wanted to make sense, not merely of all human experience of change, but of change in the inorganic world from atom to cosmos as well.

Spencer's work and its reception illustrate very well the excitement with which nineteenth-century men discovered that they were living in a world in which there could be only one rule: all things will change. Spencer grew up in a provincial town that had been becoming increasingly industrialized for some decades before his birth. During his childhood and adolescence the process continued: Derby was a microcosm of all England. Every day, it seemed, new possibilities for human existence were being opened. To a considerable extent, then, it is not surprising that Spencer saw his task as the explanation of change in all its forms. The experience of change in his own lifetime must have been extraordinarily dramatic for him and for the vast audience which turned to him for help in understanding a world going through baffling alterations. The twentieth century, steeped in the reality of change, has shown far less interest in figures such as Spengler and Toynbee, who attempted only a part of what Spencer accomplished. For the twentieth century, change might seem to come packaged into more or less neatly divided subjects: the first delirious experience of change had passed.

Spencer knew change as the most important substance of his

129

own life. His family ranked far below those of Mill or Marx or Darwin, both socially and economically. Through his talents alone he came to know Mill, Darwin, and many more of the important figures of his time. He had surpassed by far the much narrower limits of his father's life. His father, a rather hapless schoolmaster and tutor, played an important part in forming his son's ideas, because he insisted upon a very reasonable approach to the world, and because he probably harbored aspirations toward some enormous kind of achievement, some grandly total explanation which only his son could make real. Spencer's father was hampered by his roots in the intellectual tradition and the society of the eighteenth century, and by contradictions and inhibitions within his personality. Spencer conquered or avoided both kinds of difficulty to an impressive degree. He described his early development at length in the *Autobiography* on which he worked during the 1880s and 1890s.[1]

In the narrative of my boyhood I pointed out that I early became possessed by the idea of causation. My father's frequent questions—"Can you tell me the cause of this?" or—"I wonder what is the cause of that," presented to me now one thing and now another, as due to some identifiable agency, usually physical. Though his religious views prevented him from denying the miraculous, yet so frequently did there recur the interpretation of things as natural, and so little reference did he make to the supernatural, that there grew up in me a tacit belief that whatever occurred had its assignable cause of a comprehensible kind. Such notions as uniformity of law and an established order, were of course not then entertained; but the kind of thinking into which I had been led, and which was in part natural to me, prepared the way for acceptance of such notions in due time. . . . Doubtless my intellectual leaning towards belief in natural causation everywhere operating, and my consequent tendency to disbelieve alleged miracles, had much to do with my gradual relinquishment of the current creed and its associated story of creation—a relinquishment which went on insensibly during early manhood. Doubtless, too,

[1] *An Autobiography* (New York: D. Appleton and Company, 1904), II, 6-7.

a belief in evolution at large was then latent; since, little as the fact is recognized, anyone who, abandoning the supernaturalism of theology, accepts in full the naturalism of science, tacitly asserts that all things as they now exist have been evolved. . . .

Let Men Change Their Own Lives!

The idea of dissent and the importance of being different dominated Spencer's family. In religion his parents were dissenters from the established Church of England, his mother devoutly Methodist, his father occasionally attending Quaker meetings and sometimes almost estranged from any kind of religion. As Spencer remembered his father and his uncles, they were always ready to argue about any position, and it took only a statement of a positive view of any sort to trigger their combative disagreement. In his *Autobiography* Spencer offered a striking example of their effect on him. When he read Sir Charles Lyell's attack on the hypothesis of development, in which Lyell argued that change was constant but not progressive, he turned readily to that hypothesis. If Lyell was against it, then he must be for it. Authoritative figures and the whole concept of being an authority always created extreme difficulties for Spencer, painfully evident in the squabbles about priority frequent in his later life. That Spencer's habitual dissent had some irrational roots is quite probable; that it also supported his conviction that he was right in his great vision that change was understandable—but only by him—is also very likely.

Spencer had no university education, a lack that was far from tragic, considering the state of English universities in the earlier nineteenth century. He had very little formal schooling of any kind, and it is doubtful whether conventional education could have affected him very deeply. Furthermore, Spencer's main interest, change as a reality, was a subject almost unexplored, so that he could start off on an equal basis with most people; in this sense, he really needed little training. He resembles Darwin in being able to take from others just enough to meet his own purposes and still leave his sense of independence, and even of self-sufficiency, unimpaired. Darwin seems to have been more willing to learn something from other people, and so he escaped some of the dangers of being a self-taught thinker which helped to make Spencer's work idiosyncratic and, eventually, outmoded.

The youthful Spencer decided on a career which perfectly expressed the changeability of the world around him: he became an engineer. He obtained his training as an apprentice and assistant on the job, because the engineering profession had not yet become standardized and widespread enough to train recruits in schools. Helping to build the London and Birmingham Railway, between 1837 and 1846, he noticed more and more evidence of change: over the landscape, as lines spread out; and in Parliamentary lobbies and business offices, as new ventures were projected, to be financed in new ways with money that often came from the newly rich.

When he was still very young, Spencer experienced an intense desire to write. His father had been similarly ambitious, but never managed to finish anything. Spencer published a few papers on engineering subjects, but his real interest lay elsewhere:[2]

... In June, 1842, my thoughts on political matters resulted in the letters to *The Nonconformist* on "The Proper Sphere of Government"—a somewhat strange subject for a young man of twenty-two to enter upon. The general tenor of these letters betrays the emotional leanings. Individuality was pronounced in all members of the family, and pronounced individuality is necessarily more or less at variance with authority. A self-dependent and self-asserting nature resists all such government as is not expressive of equitable restraint. Our family was essentially a *dissenting* family; and dissent is an expression of antagonism to arbitrary control. Of course a wish to limit State-action is a natural concomitant; and this characterised the letters on "The Proper Sphere of Government." Beyond this constitutional tendency, here first illustrated, there was shown the tendency to regard social phenomena as subordinate to natural law: the two tendencies being, in an

[2] "The Filiation of Ideas," an essay which Spencer finished in 1899, is printed in David Duncan, LL.D., *Life and Letters of Herbert Spencer* (New York: D. Appleton and Company, 1908), II, 304-365. The quotation is from pp. 309-10. Reprinted by permission of Appleton-Century-Crofts, Inc.

indirect way, correlatives. Already in those early days the culture I have described had fostered the belief that in society as in the world at large, there are uniformities of relation; and national life was vaguely thought of as a life having certain similarities to life at large. Though it had not yet taken shape, there was a dim idea of a social organism.

[Spencer settled "The Proper Sphere of Government" by starting from the most general view of the universe at which he then could arrive. What would be lawful (in the sense of proper and fitting) for government or for society regarded as an organism, would follow by deduction.[3]]

Everything in nature has its laws. Inorganic matter has its dynamical properties, its chemical affinities; organic matter, more complex, more easily destroyed, has also its governing principles. . . . Man, as an animate being, has functions to perform, . . . has instincts to be obeyed . . .; and so long as he performs those functions, as he obeys those instincts, as he bends to the laws of his nature, so long does he remain in health. All disobedience to these laws, all transgression, produces its own punishment. Nature will be obeyed.

As with man viewed physically, so with man viewed spiritually. Mind has its laws as well as matter. . . .

As with man viewed individually, so with man socially. Society as certainly has its governing principles as man has. . . .

The point conceded, it follows that the whole welfare of mankind depends upon a thorough knowledge of social principles, and an entire obedience to them. . . .

The legislature is the most important of all national institutions, and as such it claims our first attention in the investigation of social laws. An attempt to arrive at first principles, from the study of existing governments, . . . would be a work of endless perplexity. . . . To obtain clear ideas we must consider the question abstractly. . . .

Let us, then, imagine a number of men living together without any recognised laws. . . . The weak . . . are opposed by the more powerful. . . . Every man, therefore, soon comes to the conclusion

[3] *The Nonconformist*, 2 (1842), 411.

that his individual interest, as well as that of the community at large, will be best served by entering into a common bond of protection. . . .

[The men who establish this bond] know, or they ought to know, that the laws of society are of such a nature that minor evils will rectify themselves; that there is in society, as in every other part of creation, that beautiful self-adjusting principle which will keep everything in equilibrium; and, moreover, that as the interference of man in external nature destroys that equilibrium, and produces greater evils than those to be remedied, so the attempt to regulate all the actions of a people by legislation will entail little else but misery and confusion.

What, then, do they want a government for? Not to regulate commerce; not to educate the people; not to teach religion; not to administer charity; not to make roads and railways; but simply to defend the natural rights of man—to protect persons and property—to prevent the aggressions of the powerful upon the weak; in a word, to administer justice. This is the natural, the original office of government; it was not intended to do less, it ought not to be allowed to do more.

[Nations which correctly limited the functions of government would make war disappear:[4]]

We are told that the time shall come when nations "shall beat their swords into ploughshares and their spears into pruning hooks." That time may yet be afar off, but we are advancing towards it—we shall eventually arrive at it, and that too, we may assure ourselves, not by any sudden revolution, but by a continued moral and intellectual progression. We ought not to wait for a direct interposition of the Almighty; we must use proper means; we must put our shoulders to the wheel, and then look for the fulfilment [sic] of the promise as the result of our obedience to the commands. But what are the means? One of them we have before us. Confine the attention of our rulers to their only duty, the administration of justice; and, as far as we are concerned, the promise is fulfilled. . . .

Suppose . . . that all nations confined the attention of their

----
[4] *The Nonconformist,* 2 (1842), 603.

governments to the administration of justice, aggressive war would cease; but when aggressive war ceases, defensive war becomes unnecessary, and no government could be required to exceed its defined duty.

[If government really ought to be doing very little, then every male could safely be given the right to vote, because exercising the franchise would require very little intelligence. Left to their own devices, men would perform far more ably than under government direction.[5]]

That the affairs of the nation are in a state of dreadful embarrassment, and that it may take some skill to bring them back to their normal condition, is not denied; but, whilst it can be shown that this disastrous state of things has resulted—not from want of legislation, but from over[-]legislation—not from any intellectual deficiency on the part of our law makers, but from their everlasting selfish interference—the fact can afford no argument against complete suffrage. . . .

Our state physicians have, from time immemorial, persuaded the people that social affairs would never go right without their interference; that the ever-clashing interests of different grades of men required regulation; that a vigilant supervision was necessary to secure the healthy fulfillment of all the national functions; and, in accordance with all these notions, they have been for ever doctoring the affairs of the country, now prescribing a lower diet under the name of "restrictive duties," and then allowing a surfeit of food to make up for past privations—at one time administering a stimulus to exercise, styled "encouragement to home manufactures," and at another raising an outcry for some remedy against over-production—here providing a tonic for the nation's morals, called a "national church," and there creating a war, to prevent those morals acquiring undue strength—on one part of the social body, applying a soothing ointment, in the shape of a "poor law," and on another, inflicting an extensive bleeding, under the form of an "income tax." And when, after all these transcendently skilful operations, the nation has been brought almost to the brink of dissolution—when its debility is showing itself in the most alarming forms—when its constitution is so weakened that it is hardly pos-

---

[5] *The Nonconformist,* 2 (1842), 827.

sible to cure one of its maladies without producing a worse—when, in short, it is in the state in which we now see it, we hear these sage and self-complacent legislators exclaim, "See what a difficult thing it is to govern a country!"

[Many of the ideas in "The Proper Sphere of Government" persisted as fundamental concepts in Spencer's work to the end of his life. In his early twenties he already felt very strongly that he had to spend his life saying something, and he soon knew that he had something to say. His exuberant confidence took such forms as the following statement of aims for a new periodical that was to be called *The Philosopher*:[6]]

The signs of the times are indicating the near approach of that era of civilisation when men shall have shaken off the soul-debasing shackles of prejudice. The human race is not for ever to be misruled by the random dictates of unbridled passion. The long acknowledged rationality of man and the obvious corollary that he is to be guided by his reason rather than by his feelings, is at length obtaining a practical recognition. On every hand and from every rank is springing up that healthful spirit of enquiry which brooks not the control of mere antiquated authority, and something more than the absolute dicta of the learned will henceforth be required to satisfy the minds of the people. Respect for precedent is on the wane, and that veneration heretofore bestowed upon unmeaning custom is now being rapidly transferred to objects more worthy its regard—here manifesting itself in an increased zeal for the discovery of TRUTH, and there in that deep appreciation of PRINCIPLES which characterises the real reformers of the day.

[*The Philosopher* never appeared, but Spencer was not to be daunted. Becoming increasingly certain of the value of his ideas, he finally gave up engineering and supported himself, between 1848 and 1853, as a sub-editor on *The Economist*, a recently founded but already important vehicle for reporting and interpreting current affairs.

The leisure which his job made possible, and the excellent opportunity which he had in London to observe how his world was changing, encouraged him to plan his first book. That book would owe nothing to the ideas of anyone else: Spencer was determined that he must stand alone. His tender sensibilities about indebtedness for ideas sometimes led him

---

[6] Duncan, *Life and Letters*, I, 59-60.

to minimize or distort what he gained by skimming books and periodicals and through conversation with well-informed friends. He worked his way pretty much by himself to his own conclusions. In that process he often paid the price of error or incompleteness because he was so intent on remaining unaffected by the thought of other men who would, he feared, demand a share of his glory in return for their help.

At the end of Spencer's life, Leslie Stephen remarked that although Spencer had never taken a university degree, he must have known as much as a superior graduate. Spencer replied:[7]

Your assumption is a very natural one, but it is utterly mistaken. When *Social Statics* [1850] was written I had none of that preparation which you suppose.

When with my uncle, from thirteen to sixteen, my acquirements were limited to Euclid, algebra, trigonometry, mechanics, and the first part of Newton's *Principia*. To this equipment I never added. During my eight years of engineering life I read next to nothing—even of professional literature. Then as always, I was an impatient reader and read nothing continuously except novels and travels, and of these but little. I am in fact constitutionally idle. I doubt whether during all these years I ever read any serious book for an hour at a stretch. You may judge of my condition with regard to knowledge from the fact that during all my life up to the time *Social Statics* was written, there had been a copy of Locke on my father's shelves which I never read—I am not certain that I ever took it down. And the same holds of all other books of philosophical kinds. . . . When twenty-four I met with a translation of Kant and read the first few pages. Forthwith, rejecting his doctrine of Time and Space, I read no further. My ignorance of ancient philosophical writers was absolute. . . . In 1852, a present of Mill's *Logic* having been made to me by George Eliot, I read that through: one result being that I made an attack upon one of his doctrines in the *Westminster*. . . .

[In *Social Statics* (1850) Spencer used the strategy which he had sketched in "The Proper Sphere of Government." Any decision about a course of action could be made wisely only if that course of action was considered as a particular case to which universal laws applied. These laws might be reached inductively, by sifting mountains of data. It was much more likely,

[7] Duncan, *Life and Letters*, II, 145-47. The letter was written in 1899.

however, that such sifting would yield only tendencies. How, then, could one advance beyond relying on tendencies which would only probably hold true? On the other hand, the correctness of consequences deduced from a universal law, and especially from a universal law stated in terms of physical quantities, would be incontrovertible.

Spencer was struggling with the same problem which beset Mill, Marx, and Darwin. No tendency derived from inspecting records of past change could be as certain as the workings of a law assumed to be wholly certain. Spencer, like Mill and Marx especially, wanted to make development synonymous with improvement. In *Social Statics* he rapidly deduced "The Evanescence of Evil:" [8]]

Concerning the present position of the human race, we must therefore say that man needed one moral constitution to fit him for his original state; that he needs another to fit him for his present state; and that he has been, is, and will long continue to be in process of adaptation. By the term *civilization* we signify the adaptation that has already taken place. The changes that constitute *progress* are the successive steps of the transition. And the belief in human perfectibility merely amounts to the belief that in virtue of this process man will eventually become completely suited to his mode of life.

If there be any conclusiveness in the foregoing arguments, such a faith is well founded. As commonly supported by evidence drawn from history, it cannot be considered indisputable. The inference that as advancement has been hitherto the rule it will be the rule henceforth, may be called a plausible speculation. But when it is shown that this advancement is due to the working of a universal law, and that in virtue of that law it must continue until the state we call perfection is reached, then the advent of such a state is removed out of the region of probability into that of certainty. If anyone demurs to this, let him point out the error. Here are the several steps of the argument.

All imperfection is unfitness to the conditions of existence.

This unfitness must consist either in having a faculty or faculties in excess, or in having a faculty or faculties deficient, or in both.

A faculty in excess is one to which the conditions of existence

[8] *Social Statics* (New York: Robert Schalkenbach Foundation, 1954), pp. 58-60. This is a reprint of the first edition.

do not afford full exercise; and a faculty that is deficient is one from which the conditions of existence demand more than it can perform.

But it is an essential principle of life that a faculty to which circumstances do not allow full exercise diminishes, and that a faculty on which circumstances make excessive demands increases.

And so long as this excess and this deficiency continue, there must continue decrease on the one hand and growth on the other.

Finally, all excess and all deficiency must disappear; that is, all unfitness must disappear; that is, all imperfection must disappear.

Thus the ultimate development of the ideal man is logically certain—as certain as any conclusion in which we place the most implicit faith; for instance, that all men will die. For why do we infer that all men will die? Simply because, in an immense number of past experiences, death has uniformly occurred. Similarly, then, as the experiences of all people in all times—experiences that are embodied in maxims, proverbs, and moral precepts, and that are illustrated in biographies and histories—go to prove that organs, faculties, powers, capacities, or whatever else we call them grow by use and diminish from disuse, it is inferred that they will continue to do so. And if this inference is unquestionable, then is the one above deduced from it—that humanity must in the end become completely adapted to its conditions—unquestionable also. . . .

[If the world was improving constantly, then men could very safely be left to lead their own lives. They would change when they had to, as they saw fit. Whatever they did would prove by necessity to be good, either directly or because it would lead men through suffering to a wiser course of action. As a result of these convictions, Spencer disdained much of what the twentieth century often equates with civilization itself, such as the provision and regulation by governmental officials of facilities for sanitation. Spencer acted far less from callousness of heart than from the sureness of his conviction that he knew what men ought to do. They ought to leave each other alone. Darwin came to a similar general conclusion, starting from a similar premise, his knowledge that some organisms survived and others perished when left to themselves.[9]]

The current ideas respecting legislative interference in sanitary matters do not seem to have taken the form of a definite theory.

[9] *Social Statics*, pp. 332-33, 337-38, 340. A footnote has been omitted.

The Eastern Medical Association of Scotland does indeed hold "that it is the duty of the state to adopt measures for protecting the health as well as the property of its subjects"; and the *Times* lately asserted that "the Privy Council is chargeable with the health of the Empire"; but no considerable political party has adopted either of these dogmas by way of a distinct confession of faith. Nevertheless, the opinions that widely prevail on questions of sewage, water supply, ventilation, and the like, fully commit their advocates to the belief these dogmas embody.

That it comes within the proper sphere of government to repress nuisances is evident. He who contaminates the atmosphere breathed by his neighbor is infringing his neighbor's rights. Men, having equal claims to the free use of the elements, having faculties which need this free use of the elements for their due exercise, and having that exercise more or less limited by whatever makes the elements more or less unusable, are obviously trespassed against by anyone who unnecessarily vitiates the elements and renders them detrimental to health, or disagreeable to the senses; and in the discharge of its function as protector, a government is obviously called upon to accord redress to those so trespassed against.

Beyond this, however, it cannot lawfully go. As already shown in several kindred cases, for a government to take from a citizen more property than is needful for the efficient defense of that citizen's rights is to infringe his rights; is, consequently, to do the opposite of what it, the government, is commissioned to do for him—or, in other words, is to do wrong. And hence all taxation for sanitary superintendence, coming, as it does, within this category, must be condemned.

This theory, of which boards of health and the like are embodiments, is not only inconsistent with our definition of state duty, but is further open to strictures similar to, and equally fatal with, those made in analogous cases. If by saying "that it is the duty of the state to adopt measures for protecting the health of its subjects" it is meant (as it *is* meant by the majority of the medical profession) that the state should interpose between quacks and those who patronize them, or between the druggist and the artisan who wants a remedy for his cold—if it is meant that to guard people against empirical treatment the state should forbid all unlicensed persons from prescribing—then the reply is that to do so is directly to violate the moral law. Men's rights are infringed by these, as much as by all other trade interferences. The invalid is at liberty to buy medicine and advice from whomsoever he pleases; the unlicensed practitioner is at liberty to sell these to whomsoever will buy. On no pretext whatever can a barrier be set up between them without the law of equal freedom being broken; and least of all may the government, whose office it is to uphold that law, become a transgressor of it. . . .

Inconvenience, suffering, and death are the penalties attached by nature to ignorance, as well as to incompetence—are also the means of remedying these. And whoso thinks he can mend matters by dissociating ignorance and its penalties lays claim to more than Divine wisdom and more than Divine benevolence. If there seems harshness in those ordinations of things which, with unfaltering firmness, punish every breach of law—if there seems harshness in those ordinations of things which visit a slip of the foot with a broken limb, which send lingering agonies to follow the inadvertent swallowing of a noxious herb, which go on quietly, age after age, giving fevers and agues to dwellers in marshes, and which now and then sweep away by pestilence tens of thousands of unhealthy livers—if there seems harshness in such ordinations, be sure it is apparent only, and not real. Partly by weeding out those of lowest development and partly by subjecting those who remain to the never-ceasing discipline of experience, nature secures the growth of a race who shall both understand the conditions of existence and be able to act up to them. It is impossible in any degree to suspend this discipline by stepping in between ignorance and its conse-quences, without, to a corresponding degree, suspending the prog-ress. If to be ignorant were as safe as to be wise, no one would become wise. And all measures which tend to put ignorance upon a par with wisdom inevitably check the growth of wisdom. Acts of Parliament to save silly people from the evils which putting faith in empirics may entail upon them do this, and are therefore bad. Unpitifying as it looks, it is best to let the foolish man suffer the appointed penalty of his foolishness. For the pain—he must bear it as well as he can; for the experience—he must treasure it up and act more rationally in future. To others as well as to himself will his case be a warning. And by multiplication of such warnings there cannot fail to be generated in all men a caution corresponding to the danger to be shunned. Are there any who desire to facilitate the process? Let them dispel error; and, provided they do this in a legitimate way, the faster they do it, the better. But to guard ignorant men against the evils of their ignorance, to divorce a cause and consequence which God has joined together, to render needless the intellect put into us for our guidance—to unhinge what is, in fact, the very mechanism of existence—must necessarily entail nothing but disasters. . . .

Of course, in so far as the severity of this process is mitigated by the spontaneous sympathy of men for each other, it is proper that it should be mitigated: albeit there is unquestionably harm done when sympathy is shown, without any regard to ultimate results. But the drawbacks hence arising are nothing like commensurate with the benefits otherwise conferred. Only when this sympathy prompts to a breach of equity; only when it originates an interference forbidden by the law of equal freedom; only when, by so doing, it suspends in some particular department of life the relationship between constitution and conditions, does it work pure evil. Then, however, it defeats its own end. Instead of diminishing suffering, it eventually increases it. It favors the multiplication of those worst fitted for existence, and, by consequence, hinders the multiplication of those best fitted for existence—leaving, as it does, less room for them. It tends to fill the world with those to whom life will bring most pain, and tends to keep out of it those to whom life will bring most pleasure. It inflicts positive misery, and prevents positive happiness.

Developing a System about Development

Spencer struggled very hard for literary success, and eventually left *The Economist* to make his way as a free-lance writer for the reviews of the day. He never married, and so did not need a very large income.

In 1852 he published a short essay on "The Development Hypothesis." He supported the notion, then fairly widely held, that change or evolution or development did take place, and that its occurrence was not very well explained by calling on God. Darwin often used the argument advanced here by Spencer.

Nineteenth-century thinkers were preoccupied with change, but they also needed a mechanism for insuring that desirable changes evident in one generation were not swept away in a ceaseless whirl and thus lost to the generation's descendants. Lacking any notion of the role of genes in heredity, they were forced to adopt other expedients. Throughout his life Spencer remained sympathetic with the speculations of the French naturalist J. B. Lamarck (1744-1829): changed basic needs led quite directly to changed habits, and characteristics thus acquired were inheritable. Soon after 1852, however, he would advance to a far more complicated view of change than the one outlined here.[10]

In a debate upon the development hypothesis, lately narrated to me by a friend, one of the disputants was described as arguing that, as in all our experience we know of no such phenomenon as the transmutation of species, it is unphilosophical to assume that transmutation of species ever takes place. Had I been present, I think that, passing over his assertion, which is open to criticism, I should have replied that, as in all our experience we have never known a species *created*, it was, by his own showing, unphilosophical to assume that any species ever had been created.

Those who cavalierly reject the theory of Lamarck and his followers, as not adequately supported by facts, seem quite to forget that their own theory is supported by no facts at all. Like the majority of men who are born to a given belief, they demand the most rigorous proof of any adverse doctrine, but assume that their doctrine needs none. Here we find scattered over the globe vegetable and animal organisms numbering, of the one kind . . . , some 320,000 species, and of the other, if we include insects, some *two millions* of species . . . ; and if to these we add the numbers of animal and vegetable species that have become extinct (bearing in mind how geological records prove that, from the earliest appearance of life down to the present time, different species have been successively replacing each other, so that the world's Flora

[10] *The Leader,* March 20, 1852, p. 280.

and Fauna have completely changed many times over), we may safely estimate the number of species that have existed, and are existing on the earth, as not less than ten millions. Well, which is the most rational theory about these ten millions of species? Is it most likely that there have been ten millions of special creations? or is it most likely that by continual modifications, due to change of circumstances, ten millions of varieties may have been produced, as varieties are being produced still? One of the two theories must be adopted. Which is most countenanced by facts?

Doubtless many will reply that they can more easily conceive ten millions of special creations to have taken place, than they can conceive that ten millions of varieties have been produced by the process of perpetual modification. All such, however, will find, on candid inquiry, that they are under an illusion. This is one of the many cases in which men do not really believe, but rather *believe they believe*. It is not that they can truly conceive ten millions of special creations to have taken place, but that they *think they can do so*. A little careful introspection will show them that they have never yet realized to themselves the creation of even *one* species. If they have formed a definite conception of the process, they will be able to answer such questions as—How is a new species constructed? and How does it make its appearance? Is it thrown down from the clouds? or must we hold to the notion that it struggles up out of the ground? Do its limbs and viscera rush together from all the points of the compass? or must we receive some such old Hebrew notion as, that God goes into a forest-cavern, and there takes clay and moulds a new creature? If they say that a new creature is produced in none of these modes, which are too absurd to be believed, then they are required to describe the mode in which a new creature *may* be produced—a mode which does *not* seem absurd; and such a mode they will find that they neither have conceived nor can conceive. . . .

And here we may perceive how much more defensible the new doctrine is than the old one. Even could the supporters of the development hypothesis merely show that the production of species by the process of modification is conceivable, they would be in a better position than their opponents. But they can do much more than this. They can show that the process of modification has effected and is effecting great changes in all organisms subject to modifying influences. Though, from the impossibility of getting at a sufficiency of facts, they are unable to trace the many phases through which any existing species has passed in arriving at its present form, or to identify the influences which caused the successive modifications, yet they can show that any existing species— animal or vegetable—when placed under conditions different from its previous ones, *immediately begins to undergo certain changes of structure fitting it for the new conditions.* They can show that in successive generations these changes continue until ultimately the new conditions become the natural ones. They can show that in cultivated plants, in domesticated animals, and in the several races of men, these changes have uniformly taken place. They can show that the degrees of difference so produced are often, as in dogs, greater than those on which distinctions of species are in other cases founded. They can show that it is a matter of dispute whether some of these modified forms *are* varieties or separate species. They can show, too, that the changes daily taking place in ourselves—the facility that attends long practice, and the loss of aptitude that begins when practice ceases—the strengthening of passions habitually gratified, and the weakening of those habitually curbed—the development of every faculty, bodily, moral, or intellectual, according to the use made of it—are all explicable on this same principle. And thus they can show that throughout all organic nature there *is* at work a modifying influence of the kind they assign as the cause of these specific differences—an influence which, though slow in its action, does, in time, if the circumstances demand it, produce marked changes—an influence which, to all appearance, would produce in the millions of years, and under the great varieties of conditions which geological records imply, any amount of change.

[Though his health declined severely after his toil on *The Principles of Psychology,* which he published in 1855, he continued to write by combining short periods of work with long intervals of restful self-pampering each day. In his effort to uncover the processes which made up change, Spencer gained considerable aid, which he often acknowledged, from the idea of the physiologist Von Baer that development proceeded from homogeneity to heterogeneity, from like to unlike. Spencer remained preoccupied with the desire to base all processes of change on a law stated in terms that would be considered the stock in trade of the physicist.

As he re-read his essays, preparing them for publication as a book, Spencer found the answer. About 1899 he remembered:[11]]

During a walk one fine Sunday morning (or perhaps it may have been New Year's Day) in the Christmas of 1857-8 I happened to stand by the side of a pool along which a gentle breeze was bringing small waves to the shore at my feet. While watching these undulations I was led to think of other undulations—other rhythms; and probably, as my manner was, remembered extreme cases—the undulations of the ether, and the rises and falls in the prices of money, shares, and commodities. In the course of the walk arose the inquiry—Is not the rhythm of motion universal? and the answer soon reached was—Yes. Presently—either forthwith or in the course of the next few days—came a much more important result. This generalisation concerning the rhythm of motion recalled the generalisation which was to have been set forth in the unwritten part of the *Principles of Psychology*—the generalisation that motion universally takes place along the line of least resistance. Moreover there had become familiar to me the doctrine of the Conservation of Force, as it was then called—in those days a novelty; and with this was joined in my mind Sir William Groves's doctrine of the correlation of the physical forces. Of course these universal principles ranged themselves alongside the two universal principles I had been recently illustrating—the instability of the homogeneous and the multiplication of effects. As, during the preceding year, I had been showing how throughout all orders of phenomena, from nebular genesis to the genesis of language, science, art, there ever goes on a change of the simple into the complex, of the uniform into the multiform, there naturally arose the thought—these various universal truths are manifestly aspects of one universal transformation. Surely, then, the proper course is thus to exhibit them—to treat astronomy, geology, biology, psychology, sociology and social products, in successive order from the evolution point of view. Evidently these universal laws of force to which conforms this unceasing redistribution of matter and motion, constitute the *nexus* of these con-

11 Duncan, *Life and Letters*, II, 327-29.

crete sciences—express a community of nature which binds them together as parts of a whole. And then came the idea of trying thus to present them. Some such thoughts they were which gave rise to my project, and which, a few days later, led to the writing out of the original programme, still extant. This I sent to my father on the 9th January, 1858.[12]

[Spencer was eager to make clear that he had arrived at his conception of a philosophical system which would exhaustively portray change before *The Origin of Species* appeared. He saved and annotated copies of letters that would prove his priority. In his autobiography he recalled his first reading of Darwin's book:[13]]

. . . That reading it gave me great satisfaction may be safely inferred. Whether there was any setoff to this great satisfaction, I cannot now say; for I have quite forgotten the ideas and feelings I had. Up to that time, or rather up to the time at which the papers by Mr. Darwin and Mr. Wallace, read before the Linnæan Society, had become known to me, I held that the sole cause of organic evolution is the inheritance of functionally-produced modifications. The *Origin of Species* made it clear to me that I was wrong; and that the larger part of the facts cannot be due to any such cause. Whether proof that what I had supposed to be the sole cause, could be at best but a part cause, gave me any annoyance, I cannot remember; nor can I remember whether I was vexed by the thought that in 1852 I had failed to carry further the idea then expressed, that among human beings the survival of those who are the select of their generation is a cause of development. . . .

[12] In reply to questions from Professor A. S. Packard, of Brown University, Providence, Spencer wrote (15 August, 1902): "I believe you are right in crediting me with the introduction of the word 'evolution.' I did not, however, introduce it in the place of 'epigenesis,' or any word of specially biological application, but as a word fit for expressing the process of evolution throughout its entire range, inorganic and organic.

"I believe the introduction of it was between 1857, when 'Progress: its Law and Cause' [was issued], and the time when the scheme for the Synthetic Philosophy was drawn up; and the adoption of it arose from the perception that 'progress' has an anthropocentric meaning, and that there needed a word free from that." [Note by D. Duncan.]

[13] *Autobiography*, II, 57.

[Spencer made public an outline of his proposed system in 1860; the last volume finally appeared in 1896. Without the support of friends and admirers he could never have finished his work. The number of his admirers grew steadily: he had indeed found an understanding of change which appealed to his time. His friends stood by him despite his frequently unbearable touchiness, and in an obituary notice of Mill he recalled:[14]]

Some seven years ago, after bearing as long as was possible the continued losses entailed on me by the publication of the *System of Philosophy*, I notified to the subscribers that I should be obliged to cease at the close of the volume then in progress. Shortly after the issue of this announcement I received from Mr. Mill a letter, in which, after expressions of regret, and after naming a plan which he wished to prosecute for reimbursing me, he went on to say:—"In the next place . . . what I propose is, that you should write the next of your treatises, and that I should guarantee the publisher against loss, *i.e.* should engage, after such length of time as may be agreed on, to make good any deficiency that may occur, not exceeding a given sum, that sum being such as the publisher may think sufficient to secure him." Now though these arrangements were of kinds that I could not bring myself to yield to, they none the less profoundly impressed me with Mr. Mill's nobility of feeling, and his anxiety to further what he regarded as a beneficial end. Such proposals would have been remarkable even had there been entire agreement of opinion. But they were the more remarkable as being made by him under the consciousness that there existed between us certain fundamental differences, openly avowed. I had, both directly and by implication, combated that form of the experiential theory of human knowledge which characterizes Mr. Mill's philosophy; in upholding Realism, I had opposed in decided ways, those metaphysical systems to which his own Idealism was closely allied; and we had long carried on a controversy respecting the test of truth, in which I had similarly attacked Mr. Mill's positions in an outspoken manner. That under such circumstances he should have volunteered his aid, and urged it upon me, as he did, on the ground that it would not imply any personal obligation, proved in him a very exceptional generosity. . . .

---

[14] *Autobiography*, II, 595-96.

The Foundations of the System

Spencer rested his gigantic system on a volume of *First Principles*. He felt that he had to begin by reconciling science and religion, surely a sign that he and his audience could not free themselves from the past without some difficulty. Measured against the weight of the rest of the system, however, this attempt did not figure very prominently. Like much of his other work, his concept of The Unknowable proved too unscientific for scientists, and insufficiently philosophical for philosophers.[15]

. . . Of old the Sun was regarded as the chariot of a god, drawn by horses. How far the idea thus grossly expressed was idealized, we need not inquire. It suffices to remark that this accounting for the apparent motion of the Sun by an agency like certain visible terrestrial agencies, reduced a daily wonder to the level of the commonest intellect. When, many centuries after, Copernicus having enunciated the heliocentric theory of the solar system, Kepler discovered that the orbits of the planets are ellipses, and that the planets describe equal areas in equal times, he concluded that in each of them there must exist a spirit to guide its movements. Here we see that with the progress of Science, there had disappeared the idea of a gross mechanical traction, such as was first assigned in the case of the Sun; but that while for the celestial motions there was substituted a less-easily conceivable force, it was still thought needful to assume personal agents as causes of the regular irregularity of the motions. When, finally, it was proved that these planetary revolutions with all their variations and disturbances, conform to one universal law—when the presiding spirits which Kepler conceived were set aside, and the force of gravitation put in their places; the change was really the abolition of an imaginable agency, and the substitution of an unimaginable one. For though the *law* of gravitation is within our mental grasp, it is impossible to realize in thought the *force* of gravitation. Newton himself confessed the force of gravita-

[15] *First Principles* (New York and London: D. Appleton and Company, 1910), pp. 88-89, 97. This is a reprint of the sixth edition, whose preface was dated 1900. Spencer originally issued *First Principles* in installments which were collected and published as a book in 1862.

tion to be incomprehensible without the intermediation of an ether; and, as we have already seen, the assumption of an ether does not help us. Thus it is with Science in general. Its progress in grouping particular relation of phenomena under laws, and these special laws under laws more and more general, is of necessity a progress to causes more and more abstract. And causes more and more abstract, are of necessity causes less and less conceivable; since the formation of an abstract conception involves the dropping of certain concrete elements of thought. Hence the most abstract conception, to which Science is slowly approaching, is one that merges into the inconceivable or unthinkable, by the dropping of all concrete elements of thought. And so is justified the assertion that the beliefs which Science has forced upon Religion, have been intrinsically more religious than those which they supplanted. . . .

By continually seeking to know and being continually thrown back with a deepened conviction of the impossiblity of knowing, we may keep alive the consciousness that it is alike our highest wisdom and our highest duty to regard that through which all things exist as The Unknowable.

[In March 1899 Spencer added a postscript to his section on The Unknowable, and there he recognized that the need to reconcile science and religion had vanished. Mill, Marx, and Darwin had also recognized that the nineteenth century must have its own understanding of change; religion, essentially the creation of ages which knew nothing of change, could hardly be expected to help in gaining that understanding. Religion had become quite optional as an aid in appraising the real nature of the world. Perhaps Spencer's reluctance to abandon completely the possibility of combining religion and a new grasp of change came partly from a desire not to hurt his very simple and very pious mother, who lived into the 1860s. Now, at the end of his own life, Spencer felt able to express directly the indifference to religion which had led so many men of his century to the work of Mill, Marx, Darwin—and Spencer.[16]]

But now let it be understood that the reader is not called on to judge respecting any of the arguments or conclusions contained in the foregoing five chapters and in the above paragraphs. The subjects on which we are about to enter are independent of the sub-

[16] *First Principles*, pp. 109-10.

jects thus far discussed; and he may reject any or all of that which has gone before, while leaving himself free to accept any or all of that which is now to come. . . .

. . . An account of the Transformation of Things, given in the pages which follow, is simply an orderly presentation of facts; and the interpretation of the facts is nothing more than a statement of the ultimate uniformities they present—the laws to which they conform. Is the reader an atheist? The exposition of these facts and these laws will neither yield support to his belief nor destroy it. Is he a pantheist? The phenomena and the inferences as now to be set forth will not force on him any incongruous implication. Does he think that God is immanent throughout all things, from concentrating nebulæ to the thoughts of poets? Then the theory to be put before him contains no disproof of that view. Does he believe in a Deity who has given unchanging laws to the Universe? Then he will find nothing at variance with his belief in an exposition of those laws and an account of the results.

[Spencer's key to the workings of change, his explanation of the way in which all things evolved, bore the imprint of mid-nineteenth-century physics:[17]]

Evolution, . . . under its primary aspect, is a change from a less coherent form to a more coherent form, consequent on the dissipation of motion and integration of matter. This is the universal process through which sensible existences, individually and as a whole, pass during the ascending halves of their histories. This proves to be a character displayed in those earliest changes which the visible Universe is supposed to have undergone, and in those latest changes which we trace in societies and the products of social life. And, throughout, the unification proceeds in several ways simultaneously.

Alike during the evolution of the Solar System, of a planet, of an organism, of a nation, there is progressive aggregation. This may be shown by the increasing density of the matter already contained in it; or by the drawing into it of matter that was before separate; or by both. But in any case it implies a loss of relative motion. At the

---

[17] *First Principles,* pp. 299-300, 367, 515-16.

same time, the parts into which the mass has divided, severally consolidate in like manner. We see this in that formation of planets and
satellites which has gone on along with the progressive concentration
of the nebula that originated the Solar System; we see it in that
growth of separate organs which advances, *pari passu,* with the
growth of each organism; we see it in that rise of special industrial
centres and special masses of population, which is associated with the
development of each society. Always more or less of local integration
accompanies the general integration. And then, beyond the increased
closeness of juxtaposition among the components of the whole, and
among the components of each part, there is increase of combination, producing mutual dependence of them. Dimly foreshadowed
as this mutual dependence is among inorganic existences, both
celestial and terrestrial, it becomes distinct among organic and super-
organic existences. From the lowest living forms upwards, the degree
of development is marked by the degree in which the several parts
constitute a co-operative assemblage—are integrated into a group of
organs that live for and by one another. The like contrast between
undeveloped and developed societies is conspicuous: there is an ever-
increasing co-ordination of parts. And the same thing holds true of
social products, as, for instance, of Science; which has become highly
integrated not only in the sense that each division is made up of
dependent propositions, but in the sense that the several divisions
cannot carry on their respective investigations without aid from one
another. . . .

*Evolution is an integration of matter and concomitant dissipation
of motion; during which the matter passes from an indefinite, inco-
herent homogeneity to a definite, coherent heterogeneity; and during
which the retained motion undergoes a parallel transformation.* . . .

Contemplated from a higher point of view, this law may be recognized as a corollary from the truth that change is universal and unceasing. From the centre of our system down to a microbe, each aggregate is subject to incident forces derived from other aggregates large
or small: even the Sun being affected by the planets. Nowhere is there
that sheltering from inner and outer influences which is implied
by absolute rest.

[Integration everywhere proceeds from like to unlike. Here Spencer describes the development of an embryo:[18]]

In the mammalian embryo the heart, at first a long pulsating blood-vessel, by and by twists upon itself and integrates. The bile-cells constituting the rudimentary liver, do not simply become different from the wall of the intestine in which they at first lie, but, while accumulating, they diverge from it and consolidate into an organ. The anterior portion of the cerebro-spinal axis, at first continuous with the rest, and not markedly distinguished from it, undergoes a union of its rapidly-growing parts; and at the same time the resulting head folds into a mass marked off from the spine. The like process, variously exhibited in other organs, is meanwhile exhibited by the body as a whole; which becomes integrated somewhat in the same way that an outspread handkerchief and its contents become integrated when its edges are drawn in and fastened to make a bundle.

[Changes in society offered no greater problems to Spencer than the embryo had presented:[19]]

In the social organism integrative changes are abundantly exemplified. Uncivilized societies display them when wandering families, such as those of Bushmen, join into tribes of considerable size. A further progress in mass results from the subjugation of weak tribes by strong ones; and in the subordination of their respective chiefs to the conquering chief. Such combinations which, among aboriginal races, are continually being formed and continually broken up, become, among superior races, relatively permanent. If we trace the stages through which our own society, or any adjacent one, has passed, we see this unification from time to time repeated on a larger scale and gaining in stability. The consequent establishment of groups of vassals bound to their respective lords; the subsequent subjection of groups of inferior nobles to dukes or earls; and the still later growth of the kindly power over dukes and earls; are so many instances of increasing consolidation. This process slowly completes itself by destroying the original lines of demarcation. And of the European nations it may be further remarked, that in the tendency

[18] *First Principles*, p. 284.
[19] *First Principles*, pp. 289-91.

to form alliances, in the restraining influences exercised by governments over one another, in the system of settling international arrangements by congresses, as well as in the weakening of commercial barriers and the increasing facilities of communication, we see the beginnings of a European federation—a still larger integration than any now established.

But it is not only in these external unions of groups with groups, and of the compound groups with one another, that the general law is exemplified. It is exemplified also in unions which take place internally, as the groups become better organized. There are two orders of these, broadly distinguishable as regulative and operative. A civilized society is made unlike a savage tribe by the establishment of regulative classes—governmental, administrative, military, ecclesiastical, legal, &c., which, while they severally have their bonds of union, constituting them sub-classes, are also held together as a general class by a certain community of privileges, of blood, of education, of intercourse. In some societies, fully developed after their particular types, this consolidation into castes, and this union among the upper castes by separation from the lower, eventually grow very decided: to be afterwards rendered less decided, only in cases of social metamorphosis caused by the industrial *régime*. The integrations seen throughout the operative or industrial organization, later in origin, are not merely of this indirect kind, but they are also direct—they show us physical approach. We have integrations consequent on the growths of adjacent parts performing like functions; as, for instance, the junction of Manchester with its calico-weaving suburbs. We have other integrations which arise when, out of several places producing a particular commodity, one gaining more and more of the business, draws to it masters and workers, and leaves the other places to dwindle; as witness the growth of the Yorkshire cloth-districts at the expense of those in the West of England; or the absorption by Staffordshire of the pottery-manufacture, and the consequent decay of establishments at Derby and elsewhere. . . .

Though evolutions of the various products of social activities cannot be said directly to exemplify the integration of matter and dissipation of motion, yet they exemplify it indirectly. . . . Alterations of structure in human beings, and concomitant alterations of structure in aggregates of human beings, jointly produce correspond-

ing alterations of structure in all those things which humanity creates. . . .

[If society made sense as a particular instance of a universal process, an understanding of language would also be gained easily:[20]]

That the great length of . . . familiar words implies low development, and that in the formation of higher languages out of lower there is a gradual integration, which reduces the polysyllables to dissyllables and monosyllables, is an inference confirmed by the history of our own language. Anglo-Saxon *steorra* has been in course of time consolidated into English *star, mona* into *moon,* and *nama* into *name.* . . .

[In the latter part of the nineteenth century there was a widespread belief that the universe would run down, like an unwinding clock, and eventually stop altogether. Spencer could not accept a curve of development leading to such an end:[21]]

. . . Does Evolution as a whole, like Evolution in detail, advance towards complete quiescence? Is that motionless state called death, which ends Evolution in organic bodies, typical of the universal death in which Evolution at large must end? . . .

To so speculative an inquiry, none but a speculative answer is to be expected. . . . The evidence presented in the heavens at large implies that while of the multitudinous aggregates of matter it presents, most are passing through those stages which must end in local rest, there are others which, having barely commenced the series of changes constituting Evolution, are on the way to become theatres of life. . . . When we contemplate our Sidereal System as a whole, certain of the great facts which science has established imply potential renewals of life, now in one region now in another; followed, possibly, at a period unimaginably remote by a more general renewal. . . .

[The universe would go on. Then a view of its processes which put them together, or synthesized them, from a few basic principles would have great value. Spencer's system came to be known as the "synthetic" philosophy, because it built larger and larger generalizations on the basis of a

[20] *First Principles*, p. 292.
[21] *First Principles*, pp. 484-85.

single law: physical force persisted and could only be redistributed. Initial expansions of that law made up *First Principles,* and the ultimate aim of the system was total synthesis, constructing a network of generalizations into which all particular instances—those studied in biology, psychology, sociology, ethics—would have to fit.[22]]

The task before us, then, is that of exhibiting the phenomena of Evolution in synthetic order. Setting out from an established ultimate principle, it has to be shown that the course of transformation among all kinds of existences, cannot but be that which we have seen it to be. It has to be shown that the re-distribution of matter and motion, *must* everywhere take place in those ways, and produce those traits, which celestial bodies, organisms, societies, alike display. And it has to be shown that in this universality of process, is traceable the same *necessity* which we find in each simplest movement around us, down to the accelerated fall of a stone or the recurrent beat of a harp-string.

In other words, the phenomena of Evolution have to be deduced from the Persistence of Force. As before said—"to this an ultimate analysis brings us down, and on this a rational synthesis must build up." This being the ultimate truth which transcends experience by underlying it, furnishes a common basis on which the widest generalizations stand; and hence these widest generalizations are to be unified by referring them to this common basis. . . .

How the Fittest Survived

When Spencer came to translate Darwin's idea of natural selection into mechanical or physical terms, as part of his synthesizing of all biology on the foundation of *First Principles,* he coined a notable phrase:[23]

Now if the individuals of a species are thus necessarily made unlike in countless ways and degrees—if in one individual the amount of energy in a particular direction is greater than in any

---

[22] *First Principles,* p. 369.
[23] *The Principles of Biology* (New York and London: D. Appleton and Company, 1910), I, 529-30. This is a reprint of the revised and enlarged edition whose preface was dated 1898. Volume I first appeared in book form in 1864, Volume II in 1867.

other individual, or if here a peculiar combination gives a resulting action which is not found elsewhere; then, among all the individuals, some will be less liable than others to have their equilibria overthrown by a particular incident force previously unexperienced. Unless the change in the environment is so violent as to be universally fatal to the species, it must affect more or less differently the slightly-different moving equilibria which the members of the species present. Inevitably some will be more stable than others when exposed to this new or altered factor. That is to say, those individuals whose functions are most out of equilibrium with the modified aggregate of external forces, will be those to die; and those will survive whose functions happen to be most nearly in equilibrium with the modified aggregate of external forces.

But this survival of the fittest[24] implies multiplication of the fittest. Out of the fittest thus multiplied there will, as before, be an overthrowing of the moving equilibrium wherever it presents the least opposing force to the new incident force. And by the continual destruction of the individuals least capable of maintaining their equilibria in presence of this new incident force, there must eventually be reached an altered type completely in equilibrium with the altered conditions.

[In dealing with sociology, or the science of society, Spencer deduced that redistribution of motion would create two main types of society, and then he found societies which did indeed correspond to these types. That he may have had some impression about the dominant forms of society before he began to deduce or synthesize from his basic principles is, of course,

[24] It will be seen that the argument naturally leads up to this expression—Survival of the Fittest—which was here used for the first time. Two years later (July, 1866) Mr. A. R. Wallace wrote to Mr. Darwin contending that it should be substituted for the expression "Natural Selection." Mr. Darwin demurred to this proposal. Among reasons for retaining his own expression he said that I had myself, in many cases, preferred it—"continually using the words Natural Selection." . . . Mr. Darwin was quite right in his statement, but not right in the motive he ascribed to me. My reason for frequently using the phrase "Natural Selection," after the date at which the phrase "Survival of the Fittest" was first used above, was that disuse of Mr. Darwin's phrase would have seemed like an endeavour to keep out of sight my own indebtedness to him, and the indebtedness of the world at large. The implied feeling has led me ever since to use the expressions Natural Selection and Survival of the Fittest with something like equal frequency. [Spencer's note.]

quite likely. A striking hypothesis still exists in his discusson of "the character of the militant type of social organization." [25]]

Certain conditions, manifest à priori, have to be fulfilled by a society fitted for preserving itself in presence of antagonist societies. To be in the highest degree efficient, the corporate action needed for preserving the corporate life must be joined in by every one. Other things equal, the fighting power will be greatest where those who cannot fight, labour exclusively to support and help those who can: an evident implication being that the working part shall be no larger than is required for these ends. . . . To satisfy these requirements, the life, the actions, and the possessions, of each individual must be held at the service of the society. . . .

Modern Dahomey and Russia, as well as ancient Peru, Egypt, and Sparta, exemplify that owning of the individual by the State in life, liberty, and goods, which is proper to a social system adapted for war. And that with changes further fitting a society for warlike activities, there spread throughout in an officialism, a dictation, and a superintendence, akin to those under which soldiers live, we are shown by imperial Rome, by imperial Germany, and by England since its late aggressive activities. . . .

The men who compose militant societies . . . must have a patriotism which regards the triumph of their society as the supreme end of action; they must possess the loyalty whence flows obedience to authority; and that they may be obedient they must have abundant faith. With faith in authority and consequent readiness to be directed, naturally goes relatively little power of initiation. The habit of seeing everything officially controlled fosters the belief that official control is everywhere needful; while a course of life which makes personal causation familiar and negatives experience of impersonal causation, produces an inability to conceive of any social processes as carried on under self-regulating arrangements. And these traits of individual nature, needful concomitants as we see of the militant type, are those which we observe in the members of actual militant societies.

[25] *The Principles of Sociology* (New York and London: D. Appleton and Company, 1910), II, 600-602. Volumes II and III reprint the text of the second edition. Volume II first appeared in book form in two parts, 1879 and 1882; Volume III first appeared in 1885 and 1896.

[Force continued to be redistributed, and so a second major type of society could be expected logically; it bore a resemblance to life as Spencer pictured it in *Social Statics*. Once men had moved into the industrial type of society, no further changes of comparable importance were to be expected, or should be expected, if men really understood their proper roles in the universe.[26]]

The continued existence of a society implies, first, that it shall not be destroyed bodily by foreign foes, and implies, second, that it shall not be destroyed in detail by failure of its members to support and propagate themselves. If danger of destruction from the first cause ceases, there remains only danger of destruction from the second cause. Sustentation of the society will now be achieved by the self-sustentation and multiplication of its units. If his own welfare and the welfare of his offspring is fully achieved by each, the welfare of the society is by implication achieved. Comparatively little corporate activity is now required. Each man may maintain himself by labour, may exchange his products for the products of others, may give aid and receive payment, may enter into this or that combination for carrying on an undertaking, small or great, without the direction of the society as a whole. The remaining end to be achieved by public action is to keep private actions within due bounds; and the amount of public action needed for this becomes small in proportion as private actions become duly self-bounded. . . .

For it is clear that, other things equal, a society in which life, liberty, and property, are secure, and all interests justly regarded, must prosper more than one in which they are not; and, consequently, among competing industrial societies, there must be a gradual replacing of those in which personal rights are imperfectly maintained, by those in which they are perfectly maintained. So that by survival of the fittest must be produced a social type in which individual claims, considered as sacred, are trenched on by the State no further than is requisite to pay the cost of maintaining them, or rather, of arbitrating among them. For the aggressiveness of nature fostered by militancy having died out, the corporate function becomes that of deciding between those conflicting claims,

[26] *Principles of Sociology*, II, 606-8, 611-13.

the equitable adjustment of which is not obvious to the persons concerned.

We have seen that the *régime* of status is in all ways proper to the militant type. It is the concomitant of that graduated subordination by which the combined action of a fighting body is achieved, and which must pervade the fighting society at large to insure its corporate action. . . . But as, with declining militancy and growing industrialism, the power and range of authority decrease while uncontrolled action increases, the relation of contract becomes general; and in the fully-developed industrial type it becomes universal.

Under this universal relation of contract when equitably administered, there arises that adjustment of benefit to effort which the arrangements of the industrial society have to achieve. If each as producer, distributor, manager, adviser, teacher, or aider of other kind, obtains from his fellows such payment for his service as its value, determined by the demand, warrants; then there results that correct apportioning of reward to merit which insures the prosperity of the superior. . . .

In the militant type, regimentation in the army is paralleled by centralized administration throughout the society at large; in the industrial type, administration, becoming decentralized, is at the same time narrowed in its range. Nearly all public organizations save that for administering justice, necessarily disappear; since they have the common character that they either aggress on the citizen by dictating his actions, or by taking from him more property than is needful for protecting him, or by both. Those who are forced to send their children to this or that school, those who have, directly or indirectly, to help in supporting a State priesthood, those from whom rates are demanded that parish officers may administer public charity, those who are taxed to provide gratis reading for people who will not save money for library subscriptions, those whose businesses are carried on under regulation by inspectors, those who have to pay the costs of State science-and-art-teaching, State emigration, &c., all have their individualities trenched upon, either by compelling them to do what they would not spontaneously do, or by taking away money which else would have furthered their private ends. Coercive arrangements of such kinds, consistent with the militant type, are inconsistent with the industrial type.

[Spencer now could justify with cosmic comprehensiveness the end of war to which he had looked forward in "The Proper Sphere of Government," more than thirty years earlier.[27]]

From war has been gained all that it had to give. The peopling of the Earth by the more powerful and intelligent races, is a benefit in great measure achieved; and what remains to be done, calls for no other agency than the quiet pressure of a spreading industrial civilization on a barbarism which slowly dwindles. That integration of simple groups into compound ones, and of these into doubly compound ones, which war has effected, until at length great nations have been produced, is a process already carried as far as seems either practicable or desirable. Empires formed of alien peoples habitually fall to pieces when the coercive power which holds them together fails; and even could they be held together, would not form harmoniously-working wholes: peaceful federation is the only further consolidation to be looked for. . . .

The System Wrecked by Change

Events transformed all of Spencer's great hopes into the bitterest of disapointments. The world which he was putting together by logical synthesis was rapidly overwhelmed by change in the realms of politics, economics, philosophy, and science.

When Marx sent Spencer the second German edition of the first volume of *Das Kapital*, Spencer replied with a brief note in the third person. After remarking that he was "obliged to Dr. Karl Marx" for the gift, he went on:[28]

. . . When, presently, Mr. Spencer comes to deal with politico-economic questions, as included in Sociology at large, Dr.

[27] *Principles of Sociology*, II, 664.
[28] Transcribed from a photocopy of the original, generously provided by the Marx-Engels-Lenin Institute, Moscow. This letter, catalogued as CPA IML (Moskau) f. I, op. 5, N 3325, is quoted by permission of the Institute and of the Internationaal Instituut voor Sociale Geschiedenis, Amsterdam.

Marx's volume will have an interest for him, but he fears that his ignorance of German will prevent him from gaining any adequate idea of its contents.

["The Near Future" glowered menacingly, and Spencer did not like what he saw of it:[29]]

Germany, already before 1870 having a highly organized military system, has since been extending and improving it. . . . For the support of its vast armaments those engaged in civil life are more and more taxed; which means that to the extent of those parts of their earnings taken by the State, they are owned by the State: their powers being used for its purposes and not for their own. . . .

And now we see why the socialistic movement has assumed such large proportions in Germany. We may understand why its theoretical expounders, Rodbertus, Marx, Lassalle, and its working advocates, Bebel, Liebknecht, Singer, and others, have raised its adherents into a body of great political importance. For the socialistic *régime* is simply another form of the bureaucratic *régime*. Military regimentation, civil regimentation, and industrial regimentation, are in their natures essentially the same: the kinship between them being otherwise shown by such facts as that while the military rulers have entertained schemes for a qualified State-socialism, the ruled have advocated the "training of the nation in arms," as at the socialistic congress at Erfurt in 1891. And when we remember how lately feudalism has died out in Germany—how little Germans have been accustomed to self-ownership and how much to ownership by others—we may understand how unobjectionable to them seems that system of ownership by others which State-socialism implies.

[France showed the worst kind of Lamarckian effects as one generation passed its faults on to the next:[30]]

Hence we see why in France, as in Germany, a scheme of social re-organization under which each citizen, while maintained by the community, is to labour for the community, has obtained so wide

[29] *Principles of Sociology*, III, 594-96.
[30] *Principles of Sociology*, III, 598.

an adhesion as to create a formidable political body—why among the French, St. Simon, Fourier, Proudhon, Cabet, Louis Blanc, Pierre Leroux, now by word and now by deed, have sought to bring about some form of communistic working and living. For the Frenchman, habituated to subordination both as soldier and as civilian, has an adapted nature. Inheriting military traditions in which he glories, and subject at school to a discipline of military strictness, he, without repugnance, accepts the idea of industrial regimentation; and does not resent the suggestion that for the sake of being taken care of he should put himself under a universal directive organization. Indeed he has in large measure done this already. . . .

[England provided no comfort as she renounced the great Liberal ideal of men free to change their own lives:[31]]

The evidence furnished by our own country strengthens the evidence furnished by France and Germany. . . .

Typical of the civil *régime* which has been spreading since the middle of the century, is the system of education by public agency, to support which, partly through general taxes and partly through local rates, certain earnings of citizens are appropriated. Not the parent but the nation is now in chief measure the owner of the child, ordering the course of its life and deciding on the things it must be taught; and the parent who disregards or disputes the nation's ownership is punished. . . .

And now we may see how congruous with these developments has been the development of socialistic ideas and sentiments. . . . Fourteen years ago socialism in England was represented by less than a score middle-class "Fabians," supported by a sprinkling of men among the working classes; while of late socialists have become so numerous that not long since they temporarily captured the trade-unions, and still get their views largely expressed in trade-union resolutions at congresses. . . .

After centuries during which coercive rule had been quietly diminishing and had been occasionally made less by violence, there was reached in the middle of our century, especially in England, a degree of individual freedom greater than ever before existed since

[31] *Principles of Sociology*, III, 599, 601-2, 607.

nations began to be formed. Men could move about as they pleased, work at what they pleased, trade with whom they pleased. But the movement which in so large a measure broke down the despotic regulations of the past, rushed on to a limit from which there has commenced a return movement. Instead of restraints and dictations of the old kinds, new kinds of restraints and dictations are being gradually imposed. Instead of the rule of powerful political classes, men are elaborating for themselves a rule of official classes, which will become equally powerful or probably more powerful—classes eventually differing from those which socialist theories contemplate, as much as the rich and proud ecclesiastical hierarchy of the middle ages differed from the groups of poor and humble missionaries out of which it grew.

[At the end of his life Spencer felt, as he had always maintained, that men must be left to their own devices. He had tried to make this truth plain to them, although he increasingly doubted whether they wanted to know the truth as he saw it. In 1895 he wrote in a letter:[32]]

If, as it would seem, you think that I have got a scheme for the future of society in my head you are altogether mistaken. Your conception of applied sociology—a bringing to bear of evolutionary principles on social organisation with a view to its improvement— is one which I do not entertain. The sole thing about which I feel confident is that no higher types of social organisation can grow until international antagonisms and, consequently, wars cease. . . . You have faith in teaching, which I have not—you believe men are going to be changed in their conduct by being shown what line of conduct is rational. I believe no such thing. Men are not rational beings, as commonly supposed. A man is a bundle of instincts, feelings, sentiments, which severally seek their gratification, and those which are in power get hold of the reason and use it to their own ends, and exclude all other sentiments and feelings from power. . . . There is no hope for the future save in the slow modification of human nature under social discipline. Not teaching, but action is the requisite cause. To have to lead generation after generation a life that is honest and sympathetic is the one indispensable thing. No adequate change of character can be pro-

[32] To J. A. Skilton. Duncan, *Life and Letters*, II, 76-77.

duced in a year, or in a generation, or in a century. All which teaching can do—all which may, perhaps, be done by a wider diffusion of principles of sociology, is the checking of retrograde action. The analogy supplied by an individual life yields the true conception. You cannot in any considerable degree change the course of individual growth and organisation—in any considerable degree antedate the stages of development. But you can, in considerable degree, by knowledge put a check upon those courses of conduct which lead to pathological states and accompanying degradations.

Any one who wishes to aid social advance should devote all his energies to showing, that no fundamental and permanent progress in social life can be made while warlike activities and the social organisation appropriate to them continue.

[In a chapter of "Reflections" which Spencer added to his autobiography, he assessed his life with greater satisfaction. Understanding change had yielded pleasure for him which somehow withstood the changes pulverizing the world he had put together.[33]]

Occasionally I have asked myself what have been the motives prompting my career—how much have they been egoistic and how much altruistic. That they have been mixed there can be no doubt. And in this case, as in most cases, it is next to impossible to separate them mentally in such way as to perceive the relations of amount among them. So deep down is the gratification which results from the consciousness of efficiency, and the further consciousness of the applause which recognized efficiency brings, that it is impossible for any one to exclude it. Certainly, in my own case, the desire for such recognition has not been absent. Yet, so far as I can remember, ambition was not the primary motive of my first efforts, nor has it been the primary motive of my larger and later efforts. The letters on *The Proper Sphere of Government* were prompted solely, I believe, by the desire to diffuse what seemed to me true views. That this was a chief motive to the rationalization and elaboration of them constituting *Social Statics,* seems implied by the fact that, had it not been for the publisher, Mr. Chapman, I should have issued the work anonymously. . . .

[33] *Autobiography,* II, 524-26.

Still, as I have said, the desire for achievement and the honour which achievement brings, have doubtless been large factors. Where I have been forestalled in the promulgation of an idea, I have unquestionably felt some annoyance; though the altruistic sentiment acting alone would have made me equally content to have it promulgated by another as by myself. . . . Nor can it be denied that, in the prosecution of my chief undertaking, I have been throughout stimulated by the desire to associate my name with an achievement. Though from the outset I have had in view the effects to be wrought on men's beliefs and courses of action—especially in respect of social affairs and governmental functions; yet the sentiment of ambition has all along been operative.

Two other prompters have had shares. There has been the immediate gratification which results from seizing and working out ideas. As I once heard a scientific friend say, the greatest satisfaction he knew was that yielded by a successful day's hunting—figuratively thus expressing the discovery of facts or truths. And it has been with me a source of continual pleasure, distinct from other pleasures, to evolve new thoughts, and to be in some sort a spectator of the way in which, under persistent contemplation, they gradually unfolded into completeness. There is a keen delight in intellectual conquest—in appropriating a portion of the unknown and bringing it within the realm of the known.

Of these two remaining prompters the other, allied to the last though distinguishable from it, is the architectonic instinct—the love of system-building, as it would be called in less complimentary language. During these thirty years it has been a source of frequent elation to see each division, and each part of a division, working out into congruity with the rest—to see each component fitting into its place, and helping to make a harmonious whole. . . .

JACOB BURCKHARDT

A Swiss historian and writer on art, Jacob Burckhardt (1818-1897) came from a devoutly Protestant family and at first intended to become a minister. He eventually decided to teach history, and spent most of his career at the University of Basel, rejecting invitations to more famous universities, maintaining that his true work consisted of teaching and public lectures in Basel, together with his writing. "On Fortune and Misfortune in History" was given first as a lecture at the close of 1871.[1]

Conservative and pessimistic, Burckhardt loathed eighteenth-century hopefulness about the possibility of change, and detested the changes which he saw everywhere about him in the nineteenth century. He was convinced that long-term appraisals of change, like those of which his contemporaries were so fond, were inescapably infected by the appraiser's bias and the predilections of his audience. Revolutionary upheavals such as the Franco-Prussian War, raging while he wrote this lecture, only strengthened his belief that study and knowledge alone afforded any consolation. Burckhardt's cautions may help heirs of the nineteenth century still struggling with that century's great problem: how to understand change which makes and re-makes all of life.

In our private lives, we are wont to regard our personal fate under the two categories "fortunate" and "unfortunate," and we transfer these categories without hesitation to history.

Yet from the outset we should feel misgivings, since, in our own affairs, our judgment may change radically with age and experience. Not until the last hour of our lives can we pronounce a final judgment on the men and things we have known, and that

[1] Jacob Burckhardt, "On Fortune and Misfortune in History," *Force and Freedom*, ed. James Hastings Nichols (New York: Meridian Books, 1955), pp. 309-27. Copyright 1943 by Pantheon Books, Inc. Reprinted by permission of Random House, Inc., and George Allen & Unwin, Ltd.

judgment may be totally different according to whether we die in our fortieth or our eightieth year. It has, moreover, no objective validity but only a subjective validity for ourselves. This is the common experience of any man whose youthful desires appear to him folly in later life.

Nevertheless, historical judgments of good and evil fortune in the past have been pronounced both on isolated events and on whole epochs and conditions of life, and it is mainly modern times that are prone to pronounce them. . . .

We . . . judge as follows:

> It was fortunate that the Greeks conquered Persia, and Rome Carthage; unfortunate that Athens was defeated by Sparta in the Peloponnesian War;
>
> unfortunate that Caesar was murdered before he had time to consolidate the Roman Empire in an adequate political form;
>
> unfortunate that in the migrations of the Germanic tribes so many of the highest creations of the human spirit perished, but fortunate that they refreshed the world with new and healthy stock;
>
> fortunate that Europe, in the eighth century, on the whole held Islam at bay;
>
> unfortunate that the German Emperors were defeated in their struggle with the Papacy and that the Church was able to develop its terrible tyranny;
>
> unfortunate that the Reformation triumphed in only half of Europe and that Protestantism was divided into two sects;
>
> fortunate that first Spain, then Louis XIV were eventually defeated in their plans for world dominion, etc.

The nearer we come to the present, of course, the more opinions diverge. We might, however, reply that this does not invalidate our right to form an opinion which, as soon as a wider survey in time enables us to assess at their true value causes and effects, events and their consequences, finds its justification.

By an optical illusion, we see happiness at certain times, in certain countries, and we deck it out with analogies from the youth of man, spring, sunrise and other metaphors. Indeed, we imagine it dwelling in a beautiful part of the country, a certain house, just as the smoke rising from a distant cottage in the evening gives us the impression of intimacy among those living there.

Whole epochs, too, are regarded as happy or unhappy. The happy ones are the so-called high epochs of man. For instance, the claim to such happiness is seriously put forward for the Periclean Age, in which it is recognized that the life of the ancient world reached its zenith in the State, society, art and poetry. . . .

All times of great destruction naturally count as eminently unhappy, since the happiness of the victor is (quite rightly) left out of account.

Judgments of this kind are characteristic of modern times and only imaginable with modern historical methods. The ancient world believed in an original golden age, with respect to which the world had steadily deteriorated. Hesiod paints the "present" age of iron in sinister tints of night. In our day, we may note a theory of perfection (so-called progress) in favor of the present and the future. Discoveries in pre-history reveal at least this much —that the pre-historical epochs of the human race were probably spent in profound torpor, half-animal fear, cannibalism, etc. In any case, those epochs which have hitherto been regarded as the youth of the individual peoples, namely those in which they can first be recognized, were actually very derivative and late epochs.

But who is, as a rule, responsible for such judgments?

They arise from a kind of literary consensus which has gradually taken shape out of the desires and arguments of the Age of Reason and the real or imagined conclusions of a number of widely read historians.

Nor do they spread haphazard. They are turned to journalistic uses as arguments for or against certain trends of the time. They form part of the fussy baggage of public opinion and, in part, bear very clearly in the very violence, not to say crudity, of their appearance, the impress of the time from which they issue. They are the deadly enemies of true historical insight.

And now we may enquire into some of their separate sources.

The most important of these is *impatience,* and it is the writer and the reader of history who are most subject to it. It supervenes when we have had to spend too long a time on a period, and the evidence—or perhaps our own effort—is inadequate to enable us to form an opinion. We wish things had moved more quickly, and would, for instance, willingly sacrifice one or two of the twenty-six dynasties of Egypt if only King Amasis and his liberal reform would at last carry the day. . . .

In short, we take sides for what our ignorance finds interesting against the tedious, as if for happiness against unhappiness. We confuse what was desirable to remote epochs (if anything was) with the pleasures of our imagination.

From time to time we try to delude ourselves with an apparently nobler explanation, but our only motive is one of retrospective impatience.

We pity for their unhappiness past ages, peoples, parties, creeds and so on which pass through long struggles for a higher good. Today we should like to see the aims with which we sympathize triumph without a struggle, and pluck victory without effort; and we transfer the same wish to the past. We pity, for instance, the Roman plebeians and the pre-Solonian Athenians in their century-long struggle with the hard-hearted patricians . . . and the pitiless debtors' law.

Yet it was only the long struggle which made victory possible and proved the vitality and great worth of the cause.

But how short-lived was the triumph, and how ready we are to side with one decadence against another! Through the victory of democracy, Athens declined into political impotence; Rome conquered Italy, and ultimately the world, at the cost of infinite suffering to the nations and great degeneration at home.

The state of mind which would like to spare the past its troubles, however, comes out most strongly in connection with the wars of religion. We are indignant that any truth (or what we regard as such) should have only been able to make headway by material force, and that it should be suppressed if that force proved inadequate. And it is true that truth infallibly sacrifices something of its purity and sanctity during prolonged struggles, owing to the worldly intentions of its representatives and devotees. Thus it seems to us a misfortune that the Reformation had to contend with a terrible material opposition and hence had to be represented by governments whose heart was in the property of the Church rather than in religion.

Yet in struggle, and in struggle alone, and not in printed polemics, does the full, complete life develop that must come of religious warfare. Only struggle makes both sides fully conscious. Only through struggle, at all times and in all questions of world history, does mankind realize what it really wants and what it can really achieve.

Firstly, Catholicism again became a religion, which it had almost ceased to be. Then men's minds were opened in a thousand directions, political life and culture were brought into all kinds of contact and contrast with the religious conflict, and ultimately the world was transformed and spiritually vastly enriched. None of these things could have come about in mere smooth obedience to the new creed.

Then comes the judgment according to *Culture*. It consists in appraising the felicity and morality of a people or a state of life in the past by the diffusion of education, of general culture and comfort in the modern sense. Here nothing stands the test and all past ages are disposed of with more or less commiseration. For a time, the "present" was literally synonymous with progress, and the result was the most ridiculous vanity, as if the world were marching toward a perfection of mind or even morality. Imperceptibly, the criterion of security, which will be discussed later, creeps in, and without security, and without the culture just described, *we*, at any rate, could not live. But a simple, strong mode of life, with the physical nobility of the race still intact, and the people perpetually on its guard against enemies and oppressors, is also culture, and possibly productive of a superior quality of feeling. Man's mind was complete early in time. And the enquiry as to "moral progress" we may justifiably leave to Buckle, who was so naïvely astonished that there is none to be found, forgetting that it is relevant to the life of the individual and not to whole epochs. If, even in bygone times, men gave their lives for each other, we have not progressed since.

Now follows the judgment by *personal taste,* under which we may group a number of factors. It regards such times and peoples as happy in and among whom precisely that element was predominant which lies nearest the heart of whoever is passing judgment. According as feeling, imagination or reason is the central value of life, the palm will go to those times and peoples in which the largest possible number of men were seriously occupied with spiritual things, or in which art and poetry were the reigning powers, and the greatest possible amount of time was free for intellectual work and contemplation, or in which the greatest number of people could earn a good livelihood and there was unimpeded activity in trade and traffic.

It would be easy to make the representatives of all these three categories realize how one-sided is their judgment, how inadequately it comprehends the whole life of the age concerned, and how intolerable, for many reasons, they themselves would have found life in that age.

Judgment by *political sympathy* is also common. To one, only republics were happy; to another, only monarchies. To one, only times of great and incessant unrest; to another, only times of calm. . . .

Even in the cases already mentioned, and more especially in the case of judgment by *culture,* the criterion of *security* creeps in. According to this judgment, the prime condition of any happiness is the subordination of private purposes to a police-protected law, the treatment of all questions of property by an impartial legal code and the most far-reaching safeguarding of profits and commerce. The whole morality of our day is to a large extent oriented toward this security, that is, the individual is relieved of the most vital decisions in the defense of house and home, in the majority of cases at any rate. And what goes beyond the power of the State is taken over by insurance, i.e., the forestalling of definite kinds of misfortune by a corresponding annual sacrifice. As soon as a livelihood or its revenues has become sufficiently valuable, the neglect to insure it is considered culpable.

Now this security was grievously lacking at many times which otherwise shine with an immortal radiance and till the end of time will hold a high place in the history of man. . . .

The Periclean Age in Athens was in every sense of the word an age in which any peaceful and prudent citizen of our time would refuse to live, in which he could not but be mortally unhappy, even if he was neither a member of the slave-majority nor a citizen of a city under the Attic hegemony, but a free man and a full citizen of Athens itself. Huge contributions levied by the State, and perpetual inquisitions into the fulfilment of duties toward the State by demagogues and sycophants, were the order of the day. Yet the Athenians of that age must have felt a plentitude of life which far outweighed any security in the world.

A very popular judgment in our day is the judgment by *greatness*. Those who pass such judgment cannot, of course, deny that great political power rapidly acquired, whether by the State or by the individual, can only be bought at the cost of untold sufferings to others. But they ennoble the character of the ruler and those about him to the utmost limit, and attribute to him the prophetic vision of all the great and good results which later came of his work. Finally, they assume that the spectacle of genius must have transfigured and made happy the people he had to deal with.

They dismiss the sufferings of the multitude with the utmost coolness as a "temporary misfortune"; they point to the undeniable fact that settled conditions, i.e., subsequent "happiness," have only been established when terrible struggles have bestowed power on one side or the other. As a rule, the origin and life of the man who applies this standard is based on conditions established in that fashion, hence his indulgence.

And now at last the common source trickling through all these judgments, and long since perceptible in them, the judgment by *egoism*. "We" judge thus and thus. It is true that somebody else, who is of the contrary opinion—perhaps out of egoism too—also says "we," while in the absolute sense as much is achieved by both as by the prayers of the individual farmer for sun or rain.

Our profound and utterly ridiculous self-seeking first regards those times as happy which are in some way akin to our nature. Further, it considers such past forces and individuals as praiseworthy on whose work our present existence and relative welfare are based.

Just as if the world and its history had existed merely for our sakes! For everyone regards all times as fulfilled in his own, and cannot see his own as one of many passing waves. If he has reason to believe that he has achieved pretty nearly everything that lay in his power, we can understand his standpoint. If he looks for change, he hopes that he will soon see it come, and may help to bring it about.

But every individual—we too—exists not for his own sake, but for the sake of all the past and all the future.

In face of this great, grave whole, the claims of peoples, times and individuals to happiness and well-being, lasting or fleeting, is of very subordinate importance, for since the life of humanity is one whole, it is only to our frail powers of perception that its fluctuations in time or place are a rise and fall, fortune and misfortune. The truth is that they are governed by a higher necessity.

We should try to rid the life of nations entirely of the word "happiness" and replace it by some other, while, as we shall see later, we cannot do without the word "unhappiness." Natural history shows us a fearful struggle for life, and that same struggle encroaches far upon the historical life of nations.

"Happiness" is a desecrated word, exhausted by common use. Supposing that there was a world plebiscite to decide on the definition of the word. How far should we get?

And above all, only the fairy-tale equates changelessness with happiness. . . .

The conception of a happiness which consists in the permanence of certain conditions is of its very nature false. The moment we set aside a primitive state, or state of nature, in which every day is like every other day, and every century like every other century, until, by some rupture, historical life begins, we must admit that permanence means paralysis and death. Only in movement, with all its pain, is life. And above all, the idea of happiness as a positive feeling is false in itself. Happiness is mere absence of pain, at best associated with a faint sense of growth.

There have been, of course, arrested peoples who present the same general picture for centuries and hence give the impression of tolerable contentment with their fate. As a rule, however, that is the product of despotism, which inevitably appears when a form of State and society has been achieved (presumably at great cost) and has to be defended against the rise of opposing forces, and with all available measures, even the most extreme. . . .

These stationary peoples and national epochs may exist in order to preserve definite spiritual, intellectual and material values from earlier times and to pass them on uncontaminated as a leaven to the future. And their calm is not absolute and deathly; it is rather of the nature of a refreshing sleep.

There are other ages, peoples, men, on the other hand, which at times spend their strength, indeed their whole strength, in rapid movement. Their importance resides in the destruction of the old and the clearing of the way for the new. But they were not made for any lasting happiness, or indeed for any passing joy, save for the short-lived rejoicing of victory. For their power of regeneration is born of perpetual discontent, which finds any halt tedious and demands to advance.

Now this striving, however important its consequences, however great its political consequences may be, actually appears in time in the garb of the most unfathomable human egoism, which must of necessity subdue others to its will and find its satisfaction in their obedience, yet which is insatiable in its thirst for obedience and admiration and claims the right to use force in all great issues.

Now evil on earth is assuredly a part of the great economy of world history. It is force, the right of the stronger over the weaker, prefigured in that struggle for life which fills all nature, the animal and the vegetable worlds, and is carried on in the early stages of humanity by murder and robbery, by the eviction, extermination or enslavement of weaker races, or of weaker peoples within the same

race, of weaker States, of weaker social classes within the same
State and people.

Yet the stronger, as such, is far from being the better. Even in
the vegetable kingdom, we can see baser and bolder species making
headway here and there. In history, however, the defeat of the noble
simply because it is in the minority is a grave danger, especially in
times ruled by a very general culture which arrogates to itself the
rights of the majority. The forces which have succumbed were perhaps nobler and better, but the victorious, though their only motive
was ambition, inaugurate a future of which they themselves have
no inkling. Only in the exemption of States from the general moral
law, which continues to be binding on the individual, can something like a premonition of it be divined.

The greatest example is offered by the Roman Empire, inau-
gurated by the most frightful methods soon after the end of the
struggle between the patricians and plebeians in the guise of the
Samnite War, and completed by the subjection of East and West
in rivers of blood.

Here, on the grand scale, we can discern a historical purpose
which is, to us at any rate, plainly apparent, namely the creation of
a common world culture, which also made possible the spread of a
world religion, both capable of being transmitted to the Teutonic
barbarians of the Völkerwanderung as the future bond of a new
Europe.

Yet from the fact that good came of evil, and relative happiness
of misery, we cannot in any way deduce that evil and misery were
not, at the outset, what they were. Every successful act of violence
is evil, and at the very least a dangerous example. But when that
act was the foundation of power, it was followed by the indefatigable
efforts of men to turn mere power into law and order. With their
healthy strength, they set to work to cure the State of violence.

And, at times, evil reigns long as evil on earth. . . . According to
Christian doctrine, the prince of this world is Satan. There is nothing more un-christian than to promise virtue a lasting reign, a
material divine reward here below, as the early Church writers did
to the Christian Emperors. Yet evil, as ruler, is of supreme importance; it is the one condition of selfless good. It would be a horrible
sight if, as a result of the consistent reward of good and punishment

of evil on this earth, all men were to behave well with an ulterior motive, for they would continue to be evil men and to nourish evil in their hearts. The time might come when men would pray Heaven for a little impunity for evildoers, simply in order that they might show their real nature once more. There is enough hypocrisy in the world as it is.

Let us now try to see whether the consolation we have divined will stand the test of a few of the most justified indictments of history.

Firstly, by no means every destruction entails regeneration. Just as the destruction of a finer vegetation may turn a land into an arid waste forever, a people which has been too brutally handled will never recover. There are (or at any rate there seem to be) absolutely destructive forces under whose hoofs no grass grows. The essential strength of Asia seems to have been permanently and forever broken by the two periods of Mongol rule. Timur in particular was horribly devastating with his pyramids of skulls and walls of lime, stone and living men. Confronted with the picture of the destroyer, as he parades his own and his people's self-seeking through the world, it is good to realize the irresistible might with which evil may at times spread over the world. In such countries, men will never again believe in right and human kindness. Yet he may have saved Europe from the Osmanlis. Imagine history without him, and Bajazet and the Hussites hurling themselves simultaneously on Germany and Italy. . . .

Even ancient times present a picture of horror when we imagine the sum of despair and misery which went to establish the old world Empires, for instance. Our deepest compassion, perhaps, would go out to those individual peoples who must have succumbed to the Kings of Persia, or even to the Kings of Assyria and Media, in their desperate struggle for independence. All the lonely royal fortresses of individual peoples (Hyrcanians, Bactrians, Sogdanians, Gedrosians) which Alexander encountered marked the scenes of ghastly last struggles, of which all knowledge has been lost. Did they fight in vain?

We feel quite differently about the peoples whose last struggle and end are known to us; that of the Lydian cities against Harpagus,

Carthage, Numantia, Jerusalem against Titus. They seem to us to have taken their place in the ranks of those who have been the teachers and examples of mankind in the one great cause—that all must be staked on the cause of the whole and that individual life is not the supreme value. And thus, of their despair, a happiness, harsh but sublime, is born for all the world. . . .

One thing, however, must be said of all great destructions: since we cannot fathom the economy of world history, we never know what would have happened if some event, however terrible, had not occurred. Instead of one wave of history which we know, another, which we do not know, would have risen; instead of one evil oppressor, perhaps one still more evil.

Yet no man of power should imagine that he can put forward for his exculpation the plea: "If we do not do it, others will." For then every crime would be justified. (Such men in any case feel no need of exculpation, but say: "What *we* do turns out well because *we* do it.")

It may be, too, that if those who succumbed had lived longer, they would no longer have seemed worthy of our compassion. A people, for instance, that succumbed early in the glorious struggle might later not have been very happy, not very civilized, early corrupted by its own iniquity and deadly to its neighbors. But, having perished in the flower of its strength, we feel toward it as we feel toward exceptional men who have died young; we imagine that, had they lived, they could not but have progressed in good fortune and greatness, while perhaps their meridian already lay behind them.

Consolation comes from another direction in the mysterious law of compensation, which becomes apparent in one point at least, namely in the increase of populations after great plagues and wars. There seems to be a total life of humanity which makes losses good.

Thus it is not certain, yet it appears to us probable, that the retreat of culture from the eastern half of the Mediterranean in the fifteenth century was made good, spiritually and materially, by the expansion overseas of the peoples of Western Europe. The accent of the world shifted.

Thus as, in the one case, another manner of death would have come instead of the one we know, in this case the vital power of the world replaces a vanished life by a new one. . . .

The theory of compensation is, after all, generally the theory of desirability in disguise, and it is and remains advisable to be exceedingly chary in the use of such consolation as is to be gained from it, since we cannot finally assess these losses and gains. Bloom and decay are certainly the common lot, but every really personal life that is cut off by violence, and (in our opinion) prematurely, must be regarded as absolutely irreplaceable, indeed as irreplaceable even by one of equal excellence. . . .

Another variant is the substitution of one branch of culture for another. In the first half of the eighteenth century, when poetry was almost completely negligible and painting half dead, music reached its sublimest heights. Yet here too there are imponderabilia which we must not play off against each other too glibly. The one thing certain is that *one* time, *one* people cannot possess everything at the same time, and that a great many talents, of themselves indeterminate, are attracted by the art that has already reached its zenith.

The most justified indictments which we seem to have the right to bring against fate are those which concern the destruction of great works of art and literature. We might possibly be ready to forgo the learning of the ancient world, the libraries of Alexandria and Pergamum; we have enough to do to cope with the learning of modern times, but we mourn for the supreme poets whose works have been lost, and the historians too represent an irreparable loss because the continuity of intellectual tradition has become fragmentary over long and important periods. But that continuity is a prime concern of man's earthly life, and a metaphysical proof of the significance of its duration, for whether a spiritual continuity existed without our knowledge, in an organ unknown to us, we cannot tell, and in any case cannot imagine it, hence we most urgently desire that the awareness of that continuity should remain living in our minds.

Yet our unfulfilled longing for the lost is worth something too. We owe to it, and to it alone, the fact that so many fragments have been rescued and pieced together by incessant study. Indeed, the worship of relics of art and the indefatigable combination of the relics of history form part of the religion of our day.

Our capacity for worship is as important as the object we worship.

It may be, too, that those great works of art had to perish in order that later art might create in freedom. For instance, if, in the fifteenth century, vast numbers of well-preserved Greek sculptures and paintings had been discovered, Leonardo, Raphael, Titian and Correggio would not have done their work, while they could, in their own way, sustain the comparison with what had been inherited from Rome. And if, after the middle of the eighteenth century, in the enthusiastic revival of philological and antiquarian studies, the lost Greek lyric poets had suddenly been rediscovered, they might well have blighted the full flowering of German poetry. It is true that, after some decades, the mass of rediscovered ancient poetry would have become assimilated with it, but the decisive moment of bloom, which never returns in its full prime, would have been irretrievably past. But enough had survived in the fifteenth century for art, and in the eighteenth for poetry, to be stimulated and not stifled.

Having reached this point, we must stop. Imperceptibly we have passed from the question of good and evil fortune to that of the survival of the human spirit, which in the end presents itself to us as the life of *one* human being. That life, as it becomes self-conscious *in* and *through* history, cannot fail in time so to fascinate the gaze of the thinking man, and the study of it so to engage his power, that the ideas of fortune and misfortune inevitably fade. "Ripeness is all." Instead of happiness, the able mind will, *nolens volens,* take knowledge as its goal. Nor does that happen from indifference to a wretchedness that may befall us too—whereby we are guarded against all pretense of cool detachment—but because we realize the blindness of our desires, since the desires of peoples and of individuals neutralize each other.

If we could shake off our individuality and contemplate the history of the immediate future with exactly the same detachment and agitation as we bring to a spectacle of nature—for instance, a storm at sea seen from land—we should perhaps experience in full con-

sciousness one of the greatest chapters in the history of the human
mind.

At a time when the illusory peace of thirty years in which we grew
up has long since utterly vanished, and a series of fresh wars seems to
be imminent;

when the established political forms of the greatest civilized peoples are tottering or changing;

when, with the spread of education and communications, the
realization and impatience of suffering is visibly and rapidly
growing;

when social institutions are being shaken to their foundations by
world movements, not to speak of all the accumulated crises which
have not yet found their issues;

it would be a marvelous spectacle—though not for contemporary
earthly beings—to follow with enlightened perception the spirit of
man as it builds its new dwelling, soaring above, yet closely bound
up with all these manifestations. Any man with such a vision in
mind would completely forget about fortune and misfortune, and
would spend his life in the quest of that knowledge.

READING LIST

The following list contains items which the editor has found helpful and stimulating, although he may differ with the point of view expressed in a particular work. An asterisk (*) before an entry indicates that the book has appeared in a paperback edition.

1. General

*Brinton, Crane, *The Shaping of Modern Thought* (Englewood Cliffs, N.J., 1963).

*Houghton, Walter E., *The Victorian Frame of Mind 1830-1870* (New Haven and London, 1957).

2. Mill

Annan, Noel, "John Stuart Mill," in *The English Mind*, ed. Hugh Sykes Davies and George Watson (Cambridge, England, 1964), pp. 219-39.

Mineka, Francis E., "The *Autobiography* and the Lady," *University of Toronto Quarterly*, XXXII (1963), 301-6.

Packe, Michael, *The Life of John Stuart Mill* (New York, 1954).

Pappe, H. O., *John Stuart Mill and the Harriet Taylor Myth* (Cambridge, England, and Melbourne, Australia, 1960).

3. Marx

* Berlin, Isaiah, *Karl Marx. His Life and Environment* (New York, 1963).

Cornu, Auguste, *The Origins of Marxian Thought* (Springfield, Illinois, 1957).

*Lichtheim, George, *Marxism. An Historical and Critical Study* (New York, 1961).

*Marx, Karl, *Early Writings,* trans. and ed. T. B. Bottomore (New York, 1963).

*————, *Selected Writings in Sociology and Social Philosophy,* trans. T. B. Bottomore, ed. Bottomore and M. Rubel (New York, 1956).

183

*Tucker, Robert C., *Philosophy and Myth in Karl Marx* (Cambridge, England, 1961).

*Wilson, Edmund, *To the Finland Station* (New York, 1940).

4. Darwin

Adler, S., "Darwin's Illness," *Nature*, CLXXXIV (1959), 1102-3.

Cannon, Walter F., "The Bases of Darwin's Achievement: A Revaluation," *Victorian Studies*, V (1961), 109-34.

Darwin, Charles, *On the Origin of Species* (Cambridge, Mass., 1964). A reprint of the first edition, with an introduction by Ernst Mayr.

————, *The Origin of Species. A Variorum Text*, ed. Morse Peckham (Philadelphia, 1958).

*de Beer, Sir Gavin, *Charles Darwin. Evolution by Natural Selection* (Garden City, N.Y., 1964).

Fleming, Donald, "The Centenary of the *Origin of Species*," *Journal of the History of Ideas*, XX (1959), 437-46.

Gruber, H. E., and V. Gruber, "The Eye of Reason. Development During the *Beagle* Voyage," *Isis*, LIII (1962), 186-200.

*Himmelfarb, Gertrude, *Darwin and the Darwinian Revolution* (Garden City, N.Y., 1959).

Huxley, Francis, "Charles Darwin: Life and Habit," *American Scholar*, 28 (1958-59), 489-99; 29 (1959-60), 85-93.

*Irvine, William, *Apes, Angels and Victorians* (New York, 1955).

Stauffer, Robert, " 'On the Origin of Species': An Unpublished Version," *Science*, 130 (1959), 1449-52.

West, Geoffrey, *Charles Darwin* (New Haven, 1938).

5. Spencer

Lakoff, Sanford A., *Equality in Political Philosophy* (Cambridge, Mass., 1964).

Medawar, P. B., "Onwards From Spencer," *Encounter*, XXI, no. 3 (1963), 35-43.

Plochmann, George Kimball, "Darwin or Spencer," *Science*, 130 (1959), 1452-56.